HERITAGE CRAFTS TODAY

Bandboxes

Bandboxes

Tips, Tools, and Techniques for Learning the Craft

EDWINA CHOLMELEY-JONES

Photography by Kevin Brett

STACKPOLE
BOOKS

Best Wishes to my long-time friend, Don, and his lovely wife, Arleen!

Edwina Cholmeley-Jones
"Winkie"
2009

Copyright ©2009 by Stackpole Books

Published by
STACKPOLE BOOKS
5067 Ritter Road
Mechanicsburg, PA 17055
www.stackpolebooks.com

Printed in China

10 9 8 7 6 5 4 3 2 1

FIRST EDITION

Cover design by Tracy Patterson

Frontispiece:
The wallpaper on this bandbox by Edwina Cholmeley-Jones is
a reproduction bearing a portrait of Charles II and Catherine
of Braganza from a 1662 fragment of a lining paper. The tree
crowns represent England, Scotland, and Ireland. The figures
are the four seasons. COLLECTION OF AMELIA D'ANGELI

Library of Congress Cataloging-in-Publication Data

Cholmeley-Jones, Edwina.
    Bandboxes : tips, tools, and techniques for learning the
craft / Edwina Cholmeley-Jones ; photography by Kevin
Brett. — 1st ed.
        p.   cm.
    Includes bibliographical references.
    ISBN-13: 978-0-8117-0503-5 (hardcover, concealed spiral
        binding)
    ISBN-10: 0-8117-0503-X (hardcover, concealed spiral
        binding)
    1. Woodwork.   2. Box making.   3. Bandboxes.   I. Title.

TT200.C56   2009
684'.08—dc22
                                            2009007269

CONTENTS

ACKNOWLEDGMENTS

Special thanks to editor Kyle Weaver, for giving me the confidence and help to complete this book; my friend Linda Brubaker, for recommending me to Kyle; and photographer Kevin Brett, for his creative insight in displaying my work for the images in this book.

My appreciation goes to the following individuals and institutions for their assistance: Claire Giblin and Maureen Lane of the Phillips Museum of Art at Franklin and Marshall College; Louise Kulp of the Shadek-Fackenthal Library at Franklin and Marshall College; Nicole R. Wagner and Donna Horst of Landis Valley Museum; and Robert Good and Randy Weit of the Lititz Museum.

I am grateful to many friends and family for generously lending my bandboxes from their collections to be featured in the book: Amelia D'Angeli, Gloria Angelozzi, Art and Jane Myers, Jane Lee, Linda Brubaker, Cathy Cholmeley-Jones, Dante Cholmeley-Jones, Dorothy Caven, and E. Carolyn Hazell.

I am indebted to my children for their encouragement and enthusiasm: Cathy, for her technical advice and preliminary editing; Montie III, for his creative and artistic ability in the process of developing the book; and Edward, for his admiration of my bandboxes and spurring me on with his wisdom, particularly his statement, "Any endeavor, to be worthwhile, requires sacrifice and hard work."

Lastly, my thanks to my husband, Montie, for being supportive and indulgent.

INTRODUCTION

Above: An assortment of bandboxes by Edwina Cholmeley-Jones.

Making bandboxes is a wonderful and satisfying craft. Bandboxes are traditionally made of pasteboard and sewn together with linen thread, and then covered with wallpaper and lined with newspaper. You can make bandboxes either by copying the shapes of antique examples or by designing your own boxes for specific items. Besides being decorative, bandboxes are very useful. They can be made in many different shapes and sizes to accommodate specific contents. The largest box I have made was for a pair of riding boots and the smallest was a bonnet box for a dollhouse.

My interest in history is what led me thirty years ago to take a class at the Landis Valley Museum in Lancaster, Pennsylvania, to learn how to reproduce nineteenth-century bandboxes. It was so enjoyable, and I was so intrigued by the unique quality and

Edwina Cholmeley-Jones at work.

historic importance of bandboxes, that I was inspired to pursue the craft and pass it on.

During the course of my career, I have supplied bandboxes to many museum shops, including the Museum of American Folk Art, Winterthur, the Brandywine River Museum, the Moravian Book and Gift Shop, and the Landis Valley Museum. One of my favorite commissions was to reproduce bandboxes for the National Park Service to be used at Independence Hall in Philadelphia. I also designed a special box to display maps for the National Park Service rangers.

I have been honored to have my bandboxes featured in various publications, including *American Country Christmas*, *McCalls Needlework and Crafts*, *House Beautiful*, and the first issue of *Women's World*. For many years, I have demonstrated bandbox making at Landis Valley Museum, and I have been teaching classes on the craft for more than twenty years at the Institute of Pennsylvania Rural Life at Landis Valley.

In this book, I provide you with the necessary instructions, techniques, and inspiration for making your own bandboxes.

A Brief History of Bandboxes

Above: *A bandbox covered by hand-block-printed wallpaper of a bird perched in a tree.* LANDIS VALLEY MUSEUM, PENNSYLVANIA HISTORICAL AND MUSEUM COMMISSION

Bandboxes originated in sixteenth-century England during the Elizabethan era, when it was fashionable for men and women to wear elaborate starched ruffs around their necks. These were stored in special boxes to keep them pristine. When the austere Puritan Oliver Cromwell came to power in 1653, he did away with this fashion. He wore a simple band with minimal lace and kept it in a box, originating the name "band-box." In America, most bandboxes were made between 1825 and 1850, although the earliest known wallpaper box was documented in the 1636 record of the estate of Sarah Dillington of Ipswich, Massachusetts.

The demand for boxes coincided with the industrialization of America. Previously, an ordinary family had few possessions, and a simple blanket chest was adequate storage for the whole family. With the advent of factories, however, more products became available. People were earning more money, enabling them to buy extra possessions, and they needed storage for them. Also during this period, new forms of transportation emerged. Steamboats, canals, and railroads made traveling easier and more affordable, causing an increased demand for luggage. Bandboxes helped fill this need.

There was such a demand for these wallpaper-covered cardboard or wooden boxes that both men and women could earn a living making them. A cottage industry developed, and wallpaper dealers sold the boxes. Individuals also made their own boxes at home to fill their particular needs. Many different sizes and shapes were made to accommodate myriad items, from thimbles and pins to gloves and bonnets to large celluloid hoop underskirts. The boxes were relatively inexpensive, with a large one costing fifty cents and a small one for as little as twelve cents.

Bandboxes are historically important because they document the development of America in the early nineteenth century. By studying the sizes and shapes of the bandboxes, one can determine the uses of the items

This bandbox from about 1830 is called "The Volunteer Firemen." PHILLIPS MUSEUM OF ART, FRANKLIN AND MARSHALL COLLEGE /PHOTO BY JOHN HERR

The hand-block-printed wallpaper covering this bandbox is dated 1828. LANDIS VALLEY MUSEUM, PENNSYLVANIA HISTORICAL AND MUSEUM COMMISSION

they held. The wallpaper coverings reflect the interests and fashions of the period when the boxes were made. They document important historic events, modes of transportation, and renowned figures. George Washington was frequently depicted on bandboxes. Napoleon is shown with the Duke of Wellington on one box, and another one shows him with his son on his lap. There are bandbox wallpapers depicting newsworthy events, such as the opening of the Erie Canal, the hot-air balloon ascent by Richard Clayton in 1835, and important public buildings, including the Merchant's Exchange, Holt's Hotel in New York City, and the Sandy Hook Lighthouse. Stagecoaches, sailing ships, steamboats, and steam locomotives were featured in many wallpaper designs, reflecting a fascination with travel.

There are fruits and flowers, acorns and pine cones, rural and hunting scenes, classical motifs, and geometrics. All categories of wildlife, including squirrels, beavers, birds, snakes, and exotic tropical animals, can be found on bandboxes.

Although hand-blocked wallpapers were being produced in America during this period, the fancier papers were imported from England and France. In 1825, a wallpaper machine using endless paper was imported from England. This made the printed wallpaper readily available and less expensive. In spite of the new machines, handmade paper continued to be used until the 1870s. Sometimes the background of the paper was machine-printed and the design was hand-blocked.

The linings inside the bandboxes are also important. Newspaper, contrasting wallpaper, white paper, ledgers, or other handwritten papers were used. Some boxes were not lined at all, because paper was scarce and not readily available to everyone. Newspaper was most desirable to use if the boxmaker could obtain it; the printer's ink helped deter moths and other insects, protecting the contents of the box. The newspaper linings are helpful in dating the boxes and they also give glimpses of what was happening when the box was made. Many include Civil War news.

The hunter with his dog is the theme of the hand-block-printed wallpaper over this bandbox. LITITZ MUSEUM, LITITZ HISTORICAL FOUNDATION

A pair of ruffed grouse are featured on the hand-block-printed wallpaper, dated 1835, on this bandbox. LANDIS VALLEY MUSEUM, PENNSYLVANIA HISTORICAL AND MUSEUM COMMISSION

A history of the craft would not be complete without mention of the pioneer bandbox maker "Aunt" Hannah Davis (1784–1863) of Jaffrey, New Hampshire. Hannah recognized the growing need for storage in the mid-nineteenth century, and she began making wooden boxes to earn a living after her parents died. She devised a way to splint wood to make it bend easily, and then invented a machine that could slice thin pieces of wood to make the sides of the bandboxes. For the tops, Hannah used sturdy pine. All of her boxes were oval and nailed (they were labeled, "Warranted Nailed") and covered with scraps of wallpaper she bartered from her neighbors. She sometimes obtained papers made especially for bandboxes, resulting in the renowned Napoleon and Wellington example. Many of her bandboxes were lined with newspapers that a farmer saved for her. Living near the textile factory towns of Manchester, New Hampshire, and Lowell, Massachusetts, Hannah sold her wares from a wagon to the market of young girls who worked in the mills.

This glove bandbox is covered with machine-printed wallpaper. LANDIS VALLEY MUSEUM, PENNSYLVANIA HISTORICAL AND MUSEUM COMMISSION

They were eager for boxes to keep their possessions nice and to use also as luggage when they returned to their hometowns on weekends. One can imagine the girls perched on a stagecoach surrounded by Aunt Hannah's beautiful bandboxes.

Although most bandboxes were made during the second quarter of the nineteenth century, they continued to be produced throughout the century. Many have survived throughout the years because they continued to provide storage, stowed away in attics.

Tools and Materials

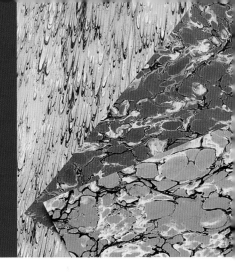

Most of the tools and materials you need for making bandboxes can be found at a craft shop or office-supply store. If you can't find what you need, refer to the Supplies and Resources section at the back of the book.

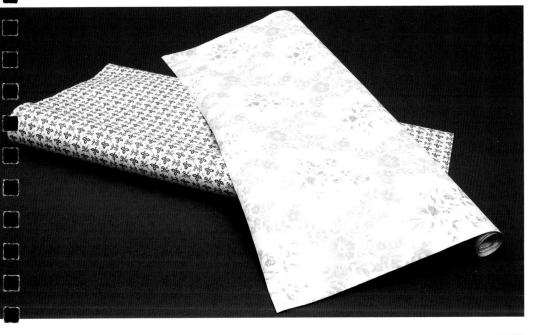

WALLPAPER OR OTHER DECORATIVE PAPER

Wallpaper is typically used to cover the outside of the bandbox. Vinyl-coated paper types are fine, but paper is easier to use. In fact, any sturdy decorative paper will work. You may want to experiment with gift wraps, endpapers from old books, or hand-stenciled papers. See the sidebar on page 36 for more ideas.

Historical gift wrap.

Marbleized papers from vintage books.

Printed marbleized paper.

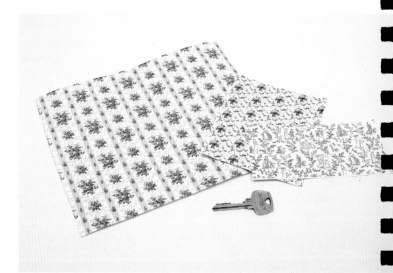

Miniature dollhouse wallpapers for small boxes.

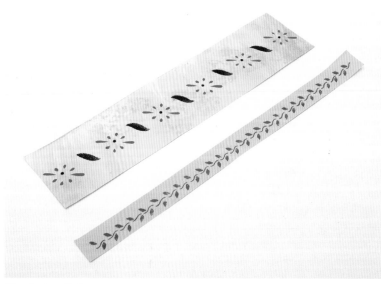

Hand-stenciled papers.

NEWSPAPER OR OTHER VINTAGE PAPER

The insides of bandboxes were traditionally lined with newspaper. To create an antique look, use vintage or historical reproduction newspaper. Other papers, such as magazine pages, sheet music, or contrasting wallpapers, can be used as well. See the sidebar on page 54.

CARDBOARD

One-ply pulpboard is the easiest to cut and sew. Pulpboard comes in 32 x 40-inch sheets. Six-ply posterboard also can be used and four-ply posterboard is recommended for tiny boxes.

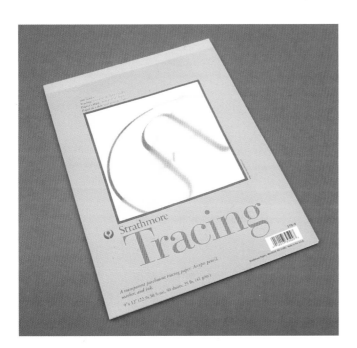

TRACING PAPER

Use standard tracing paper to trace and transfer the bandbox pattern to the pulp board.

NUMBER 2 PENCIL

You will need a soft pencil to trace and transfer the pattern to the cardboard.

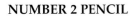

RULER AND T SQUARE

Use a ruler or T square for measuring and drawing straight edges.

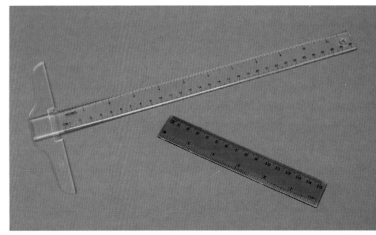

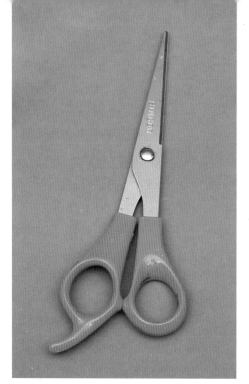

SCISSORS
Any sharp scissors will do for cutting out the cardboard.

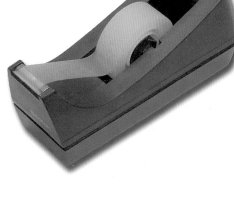

TAPE
When tracing and transferring, use masking tape or transparent tape to secure the pattern.

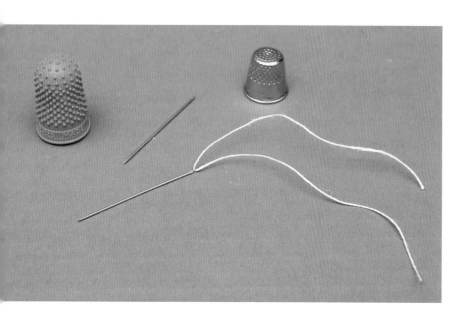

NEEDLE, FINGER PAD, AND THIMBLE
When sewing the cardboard pieces together, use a sharp needle (#5 to #7), with an eye large enough to accommodate the thread. A thimble or finger pad helps pull the needle through the cardboard.

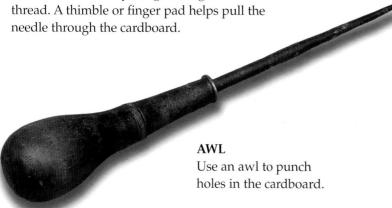

AWL
Use an awl to punch holes in the cardboard.

THREAD
For sewing, one-ply linen thread is preferred; however, any strong thread, such as button-hole, will work.

CRAFT KNIFE
Score the cardboard with a craft knife.

PAPER CLIP OR CLAMP
When punching holes in the cardboard, use a paper clip or clamp to hold the seams together.

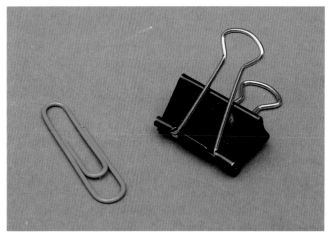

TABLESPOON AND MEASURING CUP
You will need a tablespoon to measure the dry paste and a measuring cup for the water.

BOWL
Mix the paste in a bowl.

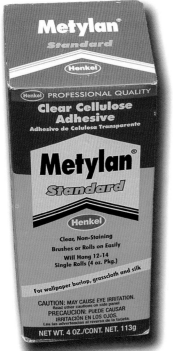

PASTE
I recommend Metylan Cellulose for pasting the wallpaper to the box. It allows you to position the paper easily on the box and can be lifted if you make a mistake. To mix, gradually add 8 ounces of water to 1 tablespoon of dry paste while stirring. Stir until water is absorbed; about 3 minutes. Let sit. The paste will be ready to use after fifteen minutes. It will last for three weeks if refrigerated.

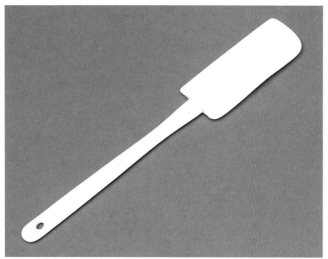

SPATULA
A spatula helps to smooth the paper, especially the inside lining.

WALLPAPER SEAM ROLLER OR BRAYER
A seam roller or brayer helps to adhere the paper to the cardboard smoothly.

BRUSH
Use a $1^1/4$-inch sponge or bristle brush to apply the paste. Larger boxes will require larger brushes.

PAPER TOWELS
Wipe away any excess paste with a paper towel.

Basic Skills

This chapter teaches the basic skills necessary for constructing bandboxes. The process will be demonstrated with an oval-shaped piece. After mastering the following skills, it will be possible for you to create the other projects in this book.

- Transferring the patterns to cardboard using tracing paper and cutting them out
- Sewing the cardboard pieces together to make the box and lid
- Measuring the wallpaper, cutting it out, and pasting it over the outside of the box
- Measuring the newspaper, cutting it out, and pasting it to line the inside of the box

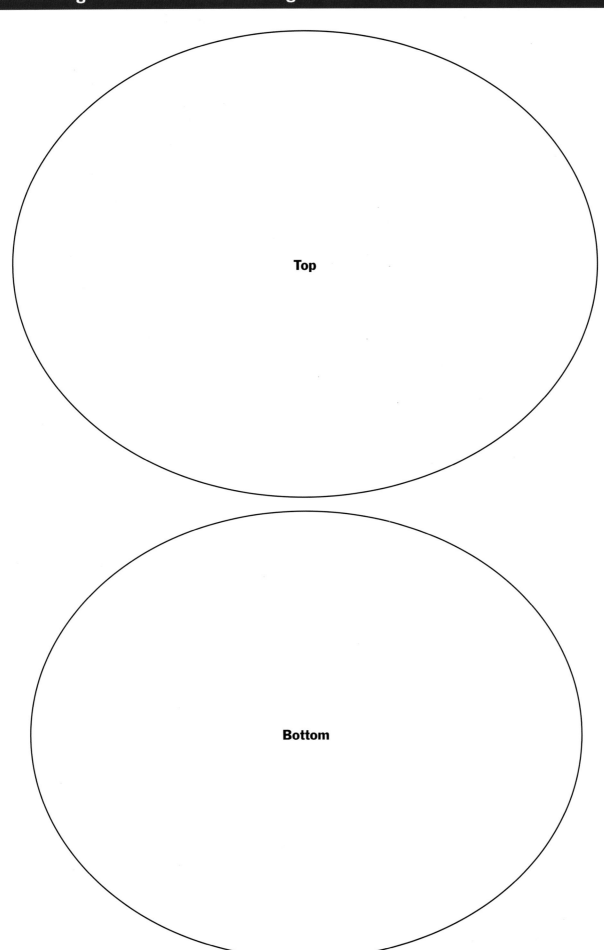

Top

Bottom

Most bandboxes are oval or round, because it is easier
and faster to sew continuously rather than stop to score
the cardboard that goes around the corners of square
and rectangle boxes.

Also Needed

- Rim: 1 x 18 inches
- Side: $3^{1}/_{2}$ x 18 inches

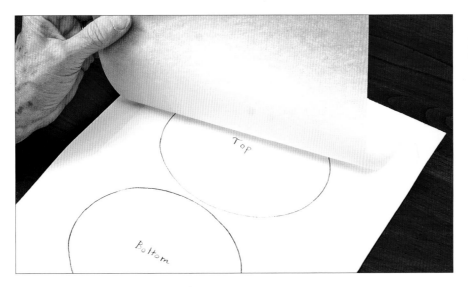

Place the tracing paper on the oval
box pattern marked TOP. Secure the
tracing paper with tape.

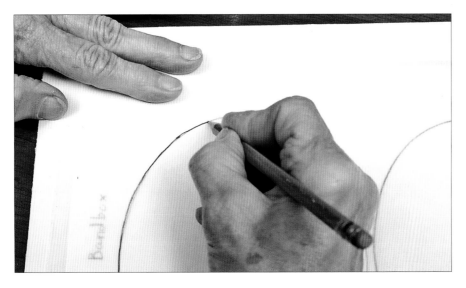

Pressing firmly with the opposite
hand, begin tracing with a number
2 pencil.

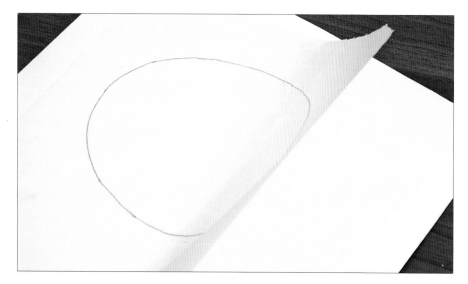

When you've finished tracing, turn the paper over.

Place the paper with the pencil-tracing side down against the pulp board and secure it with tape.

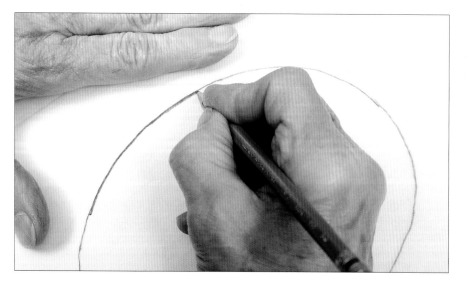

With the pencil, draw over the traced lines.

Tip

Make a cardboard template of the pattern if you plan to make multiple boxes of the same design.

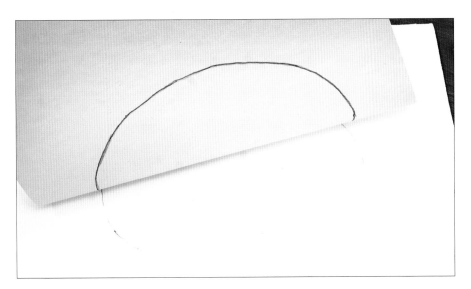

This will transfer the lines of the pattern to the pulp board. Be sure to write TOP on the tracing. Follow the same procedure for the bottom pattern and mark it BOTTOM.

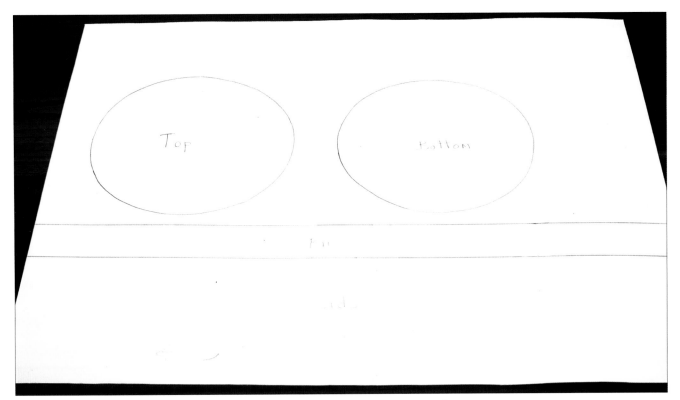

On the cardboard, measure and draw with a ruler or T square a rim piece of 1 x 18^1/$_2$ inches. Then make a side piece of 3^1/$_2$ x 18^1/$_2$ inches. Be sure to draw the rim piece and side piece along the grain of the cardboard. (The grain of the cardboard is the direction the cardboard bends without resistance.) Mark the pieces RIM and SIDE.

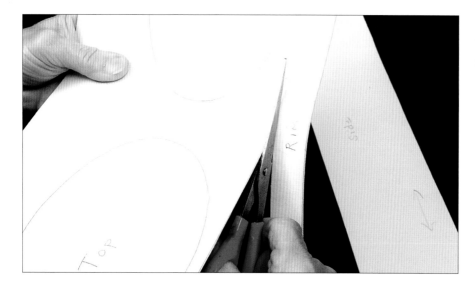

Using a sharp scissors, cut out the rim and side pieces.

Then cut out the top and bottom ovals.

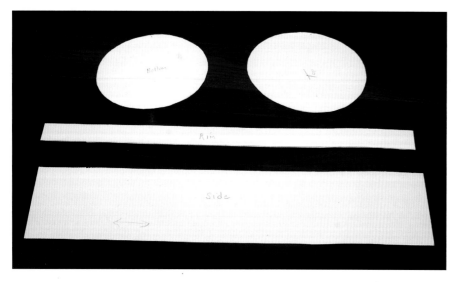

Here are the four pieces of the box.

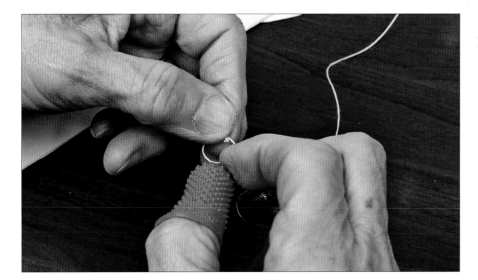

Knot a 34-inch length of thread.

Place the knot at the inside of the rim $1/4$ inch from the top edge.

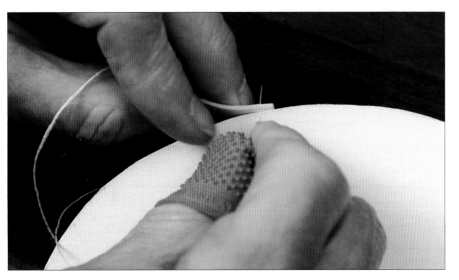

Begin sewing the rim to the top of the box. Start with one end of the rim at the middle of one side of the top, so that the ends eventually meet at what will be the back of the box. You will want all seams of the box in the back.

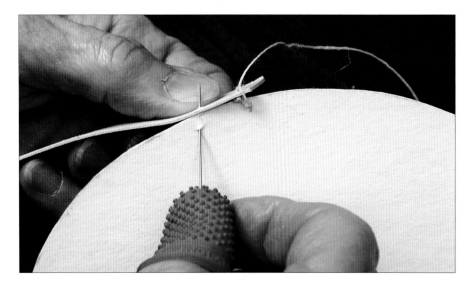

Sew the rim using an overhand stitch, which is sewing down through the top and out through the rim.

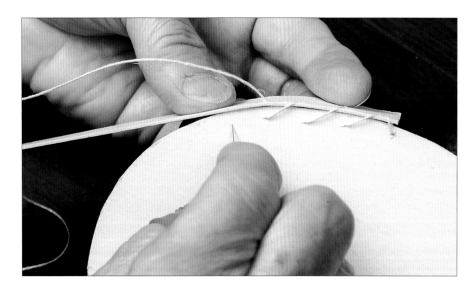

Make the stitches about $1/2$ inch apart and $1/4$ inch from the edge. Be sure the rim strip is sewn on the outside edge of the top piece to maintain the shape of the box.

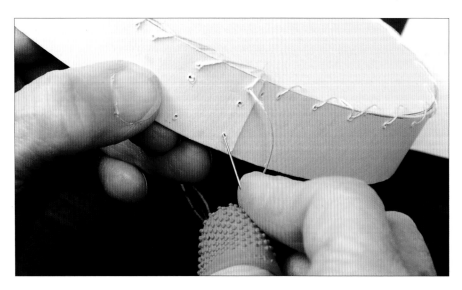

Finish by overlapping the ends of the rim piece by $3/4$ inch. Cut off any extra length. Using a needle or an awl, punch two pairs of holes on overlaps as shown.

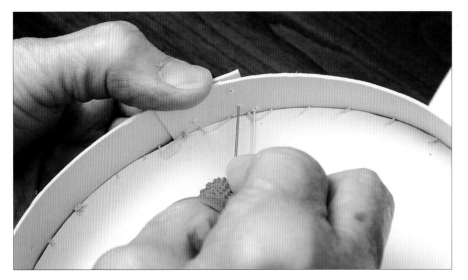

Bring the thread up through the top hole.

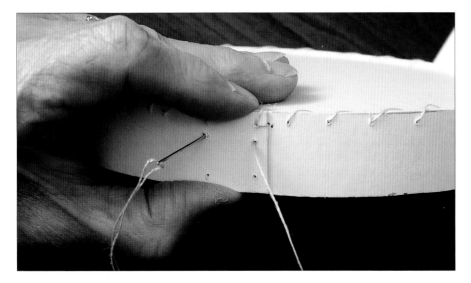

Run it across to the opposite hole.

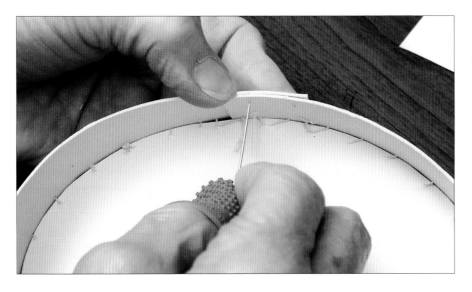

Then take it up through the bottom hole.

Move the thread horizontally to the opposite hole and go through.

Then go back across and through the adjacent hole.

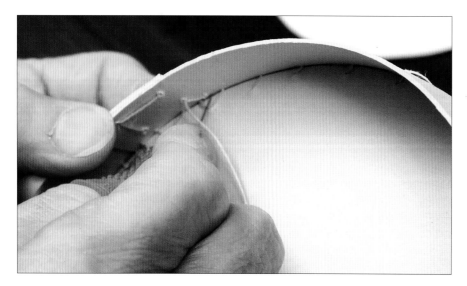

Zigzag by coming up through the opposite hole and diagonal to the top right hole.

Here is what the outside of the sewn top will look like.

Tip

If you run out of thread while sewing, go back through the last holes you stitched. This will lock the stitches in place. To join a new thread, knot it and place the knot inside at the hole where you ended.

Knot a 34-inch length of thread.

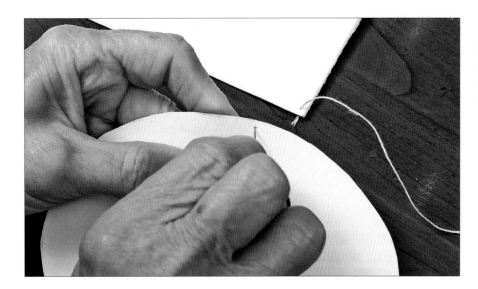

Place the knot at the inside of the side piece $1/4$ inch from the bottom edge. Begin sewing at the back of the box.

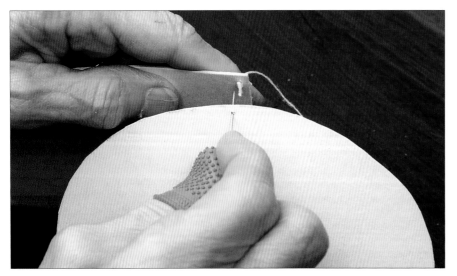

Sew down through the bottom piece.

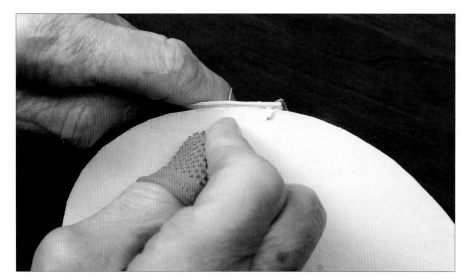

Then take the thread out through the side.

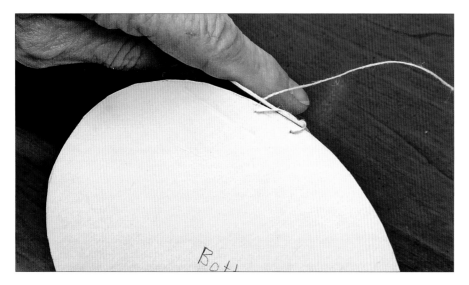

Place stitches $^1/_2$ inch apart and $^1/_4$ inch from the edge.

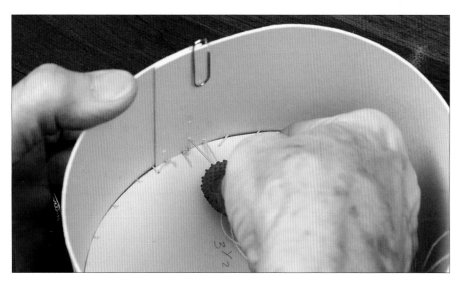

Finish by overlapping the ends of the side piece by $^3/_4$ inch. Measure to make sure the top and bottom edges overlap evenly. Cut off the excess cardboard. Use a paper clip to hold the seam together.

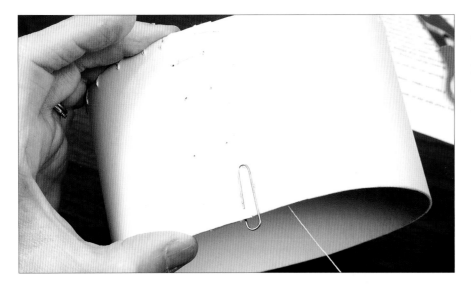

Using an awl or needle, punch four pairs of holes on the overlap. Bring the thread up through the bottom hole, across, and down the opposite hole.

Then take the thread up through the next hole.

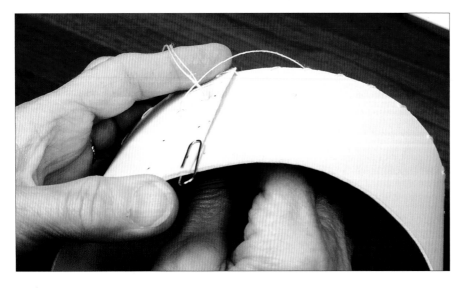

Run it down the opposite hole.

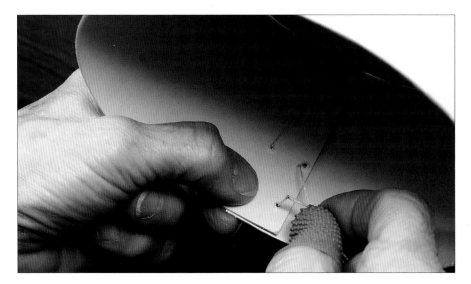

Then go up through the next hole and down the opposite hole.

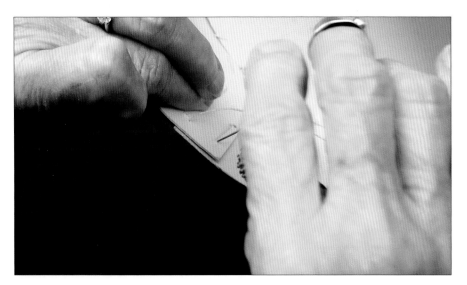

To return, go across to the opposite top hole to the outside.

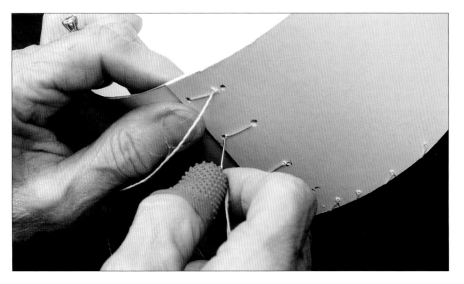

Then go diagonally to the next pair of holes, up through the opposite hole, and diagonally to the next pair of holes. Continue up through the opposite hole and diagonally to the opposite hole.

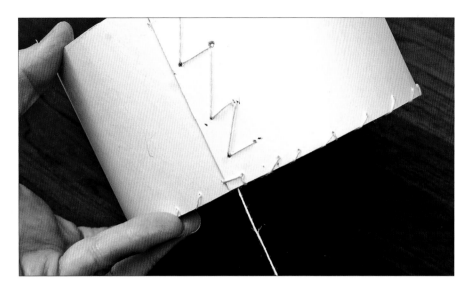

Finish by threading the needle through the opening between the bottom and the side piece.

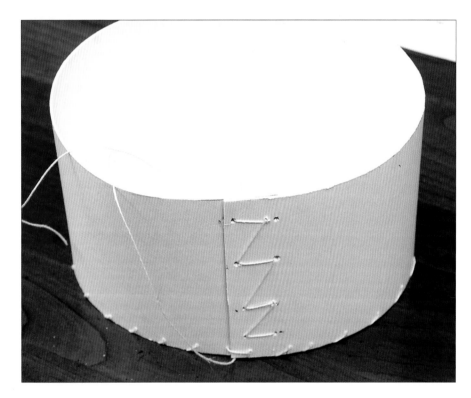

Here is the outside seam of the finished bottom piece of the box.

The box is $3^1/_2$ inches wide and $18^1/_2$ inches long. The bottom side paper covering should be $1/_2$ inch wider and 1 inch longer than the box. Measure the paper 4 x $19^1/_2$ inches.

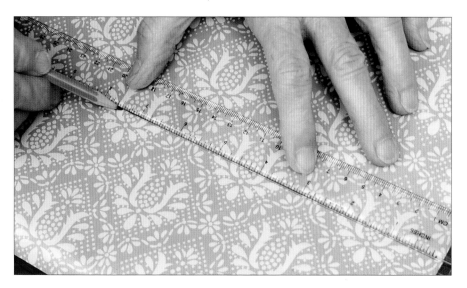

Draw a line between the measurements.

The top rim paper covering is $1/_2$ inch wider and 1 inch longer than the box. The box rim measures 1 x $18^1/_2$ inches. Measure the paper covering $1^1/_2$ x $19^1/_2$ inches.

Papers Used for Outside Covering

Bandboxes were traditionally covered with wallpaper, but you may want to try gift wraps, endpapers from old books, or hand-stenciled papers.

Hand-marbleized paper from Italy covers this bandbox by Edwina Cholmeley-Jones.

This heart-shaped box includes a fraktur design on paper, inspired by the decoration on a Pennsylvania Dutch chest by A. M. Cholmeley-Jones III.

The duck is hand-stenciled on paper and glued to the top of this bandbox by Edwina Cholmeley-Jones.

The Currier and Ives print titled *Winter* covers this bandbox by Edwina Cholmeley-Jones.

A theorem painting of fruit designed and hand-stenciled by Linda Brubaker covers the top of this bandbox by Edwina Cholmeley-Jones.

The top and bottom wallpaper is
$1/2$ inch wider all around the box.

Use the top of the box and mark the
paper $1/2$ inch larger around the box.

Use the bottom of the box to mark
the paper $1/2$ inch wider around
the box.

Cut out the wallpaper pieces and pencil in the following labels on the back of the appropriate pieces: TOP, BOTTOM, RIM, and SIDE. Here is what they look like.

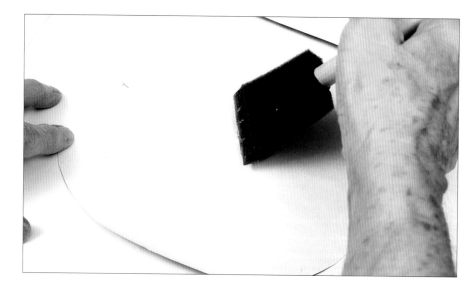

Starting with the top of the box, use a brush to apply a layer of paste to the wallpaper marked TOP.

Apply a layer of paste to the top of the box.

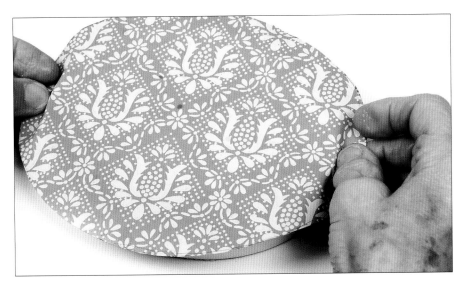

Adhere the wallpaper to the box, centering the paper so that the overlap is even all around.

Smooth the paper with a seam roller.

Roll the inside of the top.

Make sure the paper covering is smooth.

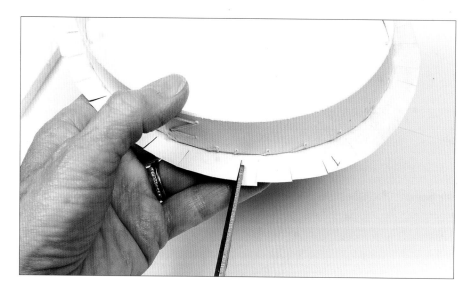

Clip around the excess paper every $1/2$ inch.

Apply paste to the top of the rim.

Fold over and press the excess paper to the rim, applying more paste if necessary.

Use the seam roller to smooth the overlap.

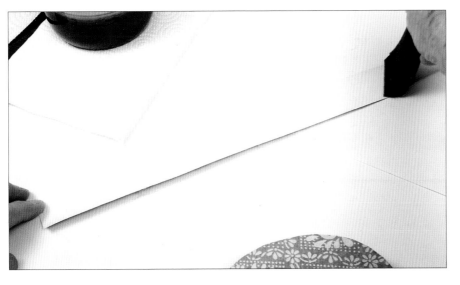

Apply paste to the rim wallpaper.

Apply paste to the box rim.

Starting at the back of the box, paste the paper rim around the rim of the box.

Overlap the paper ³/₄ inch at the seam. Trim the excess length of rim paper.

Apply paste to the overlap.

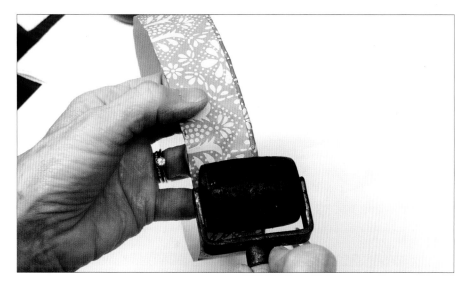

Use the roller to smooth the strip.

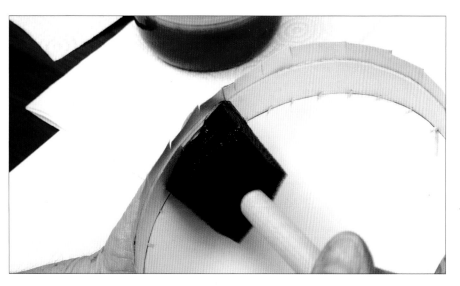

Apply paste to the inside rim.

Fold over and press the overlap paper to the inside of the rim.

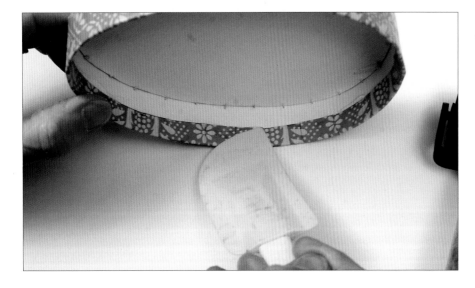

Use a spatula to smooth the inside.

Here is the finished top of the box.

Moving on to the bottom of the box, apply paste to the wallpaper marked BOTTOM.

Apply a layer of paste to the bottom of the box.

Adhere the wallpaper to the box, centering the paper so that the overlap is even all around.

Smooth the top with the seam roller.

Turn the box over and use the seam roller on the inside of the box to make the outside smooth.

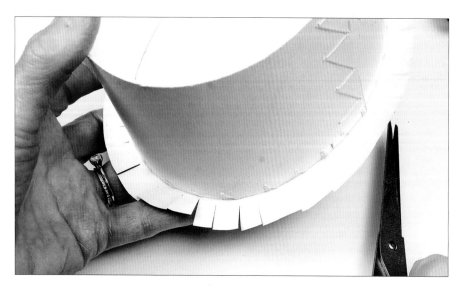

Clip the excess paper every $1/2$ inch all around the box.

Add paste to the bottom edge of the box.

Fold and press the excess paper to the side of the box, using more paste if necessary.

Smooth the side with the seam roller.

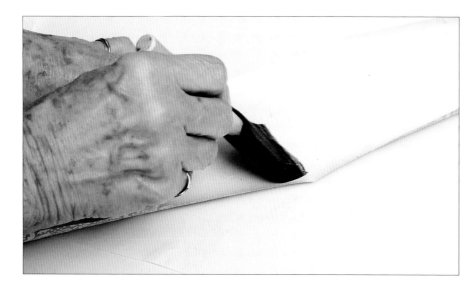

Apply paste to the back of the side wallpaper covering.

Apply paste to the box.

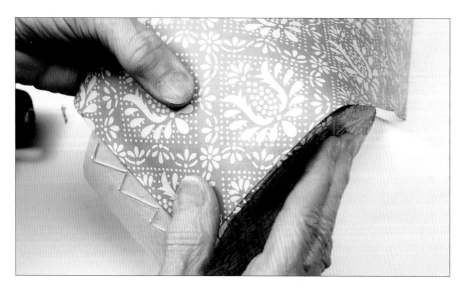

Starting at the back of the box, paste the wallpaper covering to the side of the box.

Ease the paper smoothly around the box.

Trim the excess length of wallpaper allowing for a $3/4$-inch overlap.

Apply more paste to the wallpaper so the overlap will adhere.

Roll the overlap flat.

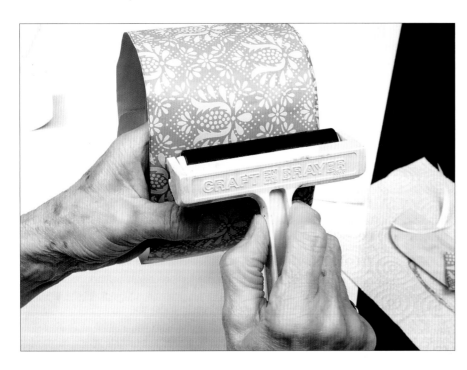

Roll the entire box to make sure the wallpaper covering is smooth.

Clip the excess width of the paper every ¹/₂ inch.

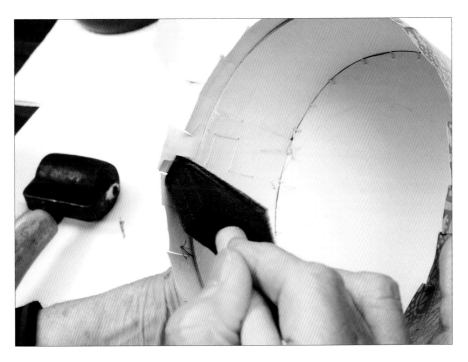

Apply paste to the inside clipped edges and to the top edge of the box. Fold over the clipped edges and press to adhere them to the inside of the box.

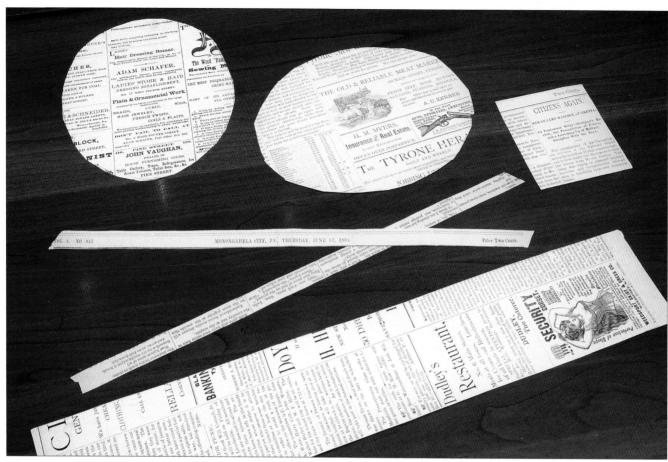

The top and bottom newspaper linings should be $1/2$ inch wider around the circumference of the actual top and bottom of the box. The box rim measures 1 x 18$1/2$ inches. The top rim lining is $1/2$ inch narrower and $1/2$ inch longer than the box rim. Measure the newspaper $1/2$ x 19$1/2$ inches. The side piece is 3$1/2$ x 18$1/2$ inches. The bottom side lining is $1/2$ inch narrower and $1/2$ inch longer than the box side piece. Measure the lining 3 x 19 inches.

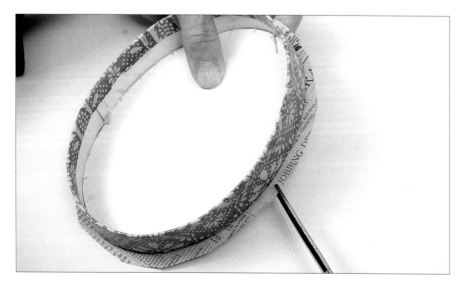

To line the top, clip the excess paper every $1/2$ inch.

Apply paste to the top piece of newspaper lining.

Apply paste to the inside top of the box.

Insert the top piece of newspaper lining into the box.

Papers Used for Inside Lining

Newspapers were typically used to line bandboxes, but other vintage papers add a nice touch.

Vintage newspaper and handscript line this bandbox, circa 1830. LANDIS VALLEY MUSEUM, PENNSYLVANIA HISTORICAL AND MUSEUM COMMISSION

Antique sheet music lines this bandbox by Edwina Cholmeley-Jones. COLLECTION OF GLORIA ANGELOZZI

A vintage magazine lines the inside of this bandbox by Dorothy Caven. It is covered with a gift wrap reproducing motifs from a late-fifteenth-century French tapestry.
COLLECTION OF GLORIA ANGELOZZI

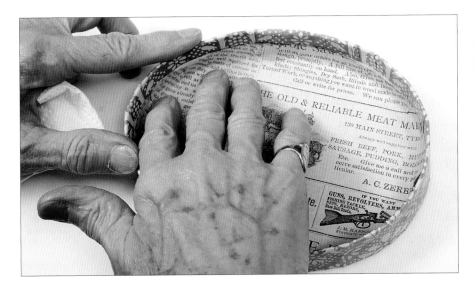

Using your fingers, fold the excess paper to the inside of the rim.

Use the seam roller to smooth.

Apply paste to the rim piece of newspaper lining.

Apply paste to the inside rim of the box.

Insert the rim piece of newspaper lining.

Overlap the end pieces.

Cut off any excess length.

Smooth it down with your fingers or a spatula.

Here is the finished inside of the top. Allow it to dry on a smooth surface. Insert a weight to make sure it dries flat for two days.

Moving on to the bottom lining, clip the extra width of the bottom piece of newspaper lining every ¹/₂ inch. Then apply paste to it.

Apply paste to the bottom of the box.

Insert the bottom piece of the newspaper lining. The clipped edges of the paper will fold up the side of the box.

Apply paste to the side piece of newspaper lining.

Apply paste to the inside of the box.

Insert the side piece of lining.

Overlap the ends of the side piece and then trim any extra length of newspaper.

Smooth the inside with a spatula. Allow it to dry on a smooth surface. The bottom usually dries flat without the insertion of a weight.

You have now completed your first bandbox.

Glove Box

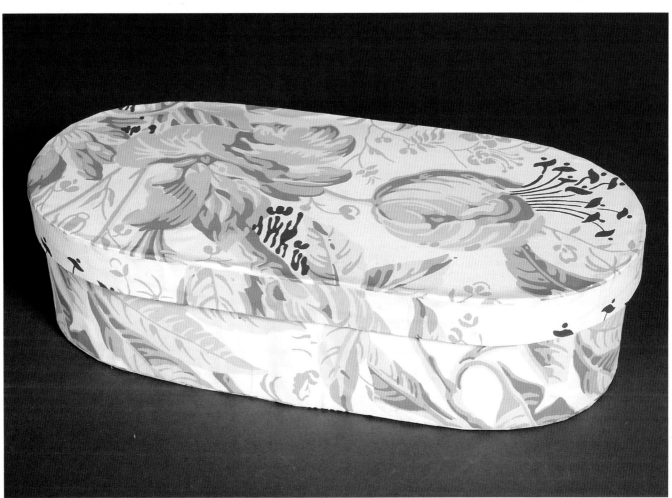

This project is a reproduction of an 1830s glove band-box. Here you will learn how to transfer a half-size pattern to cardboard to make a whole size box.

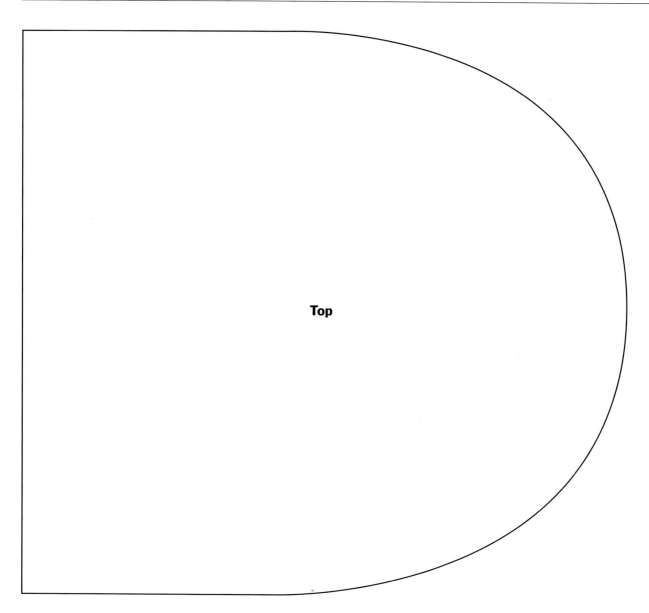

Top

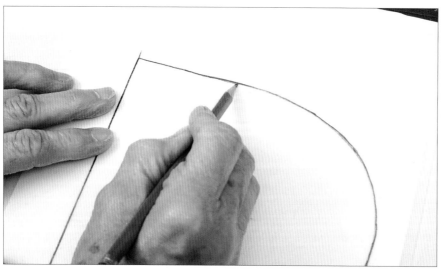

Also Needed

- Rim: $1^1/_2$ x 33 inches
- Side: 3 x 33 inches

The patterns for the top and bottom of the bandbox are only here in half form. You must trace each one again on the opposite side of the first to make a whole. With a number 2 pencil, trace the half top pattern of the glove box.

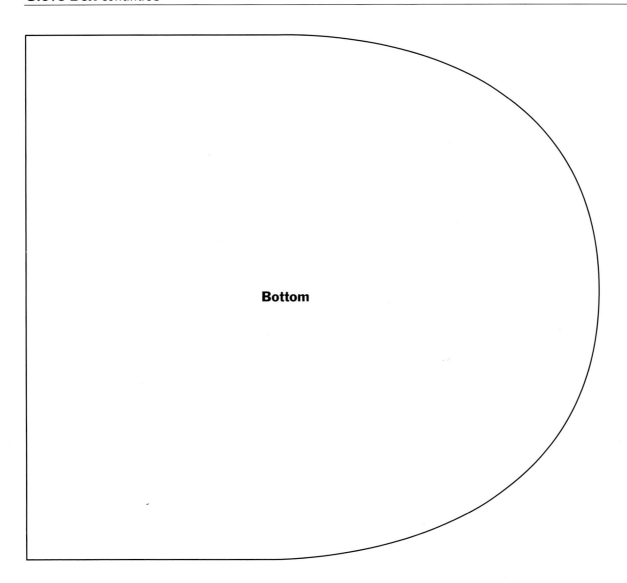

Bottom

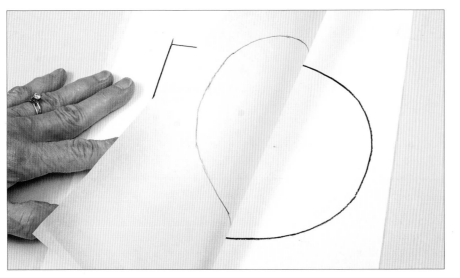

Turn the tracing paper over.

Go over the traced lines with a number 2 pencil. The pattern will be transferred to the pulp board.

Mark the center line at both edges.

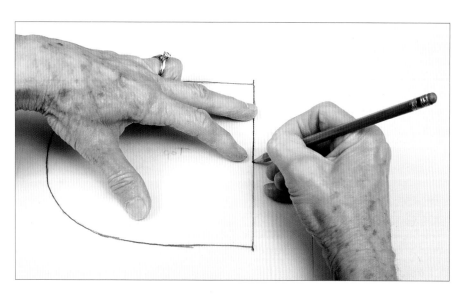

Draw a line between marks.

Turn the tracing paper over. Line up the center of the paper pattern with the center of the transferred image on the cardboard.

Tack down the transfer paper.

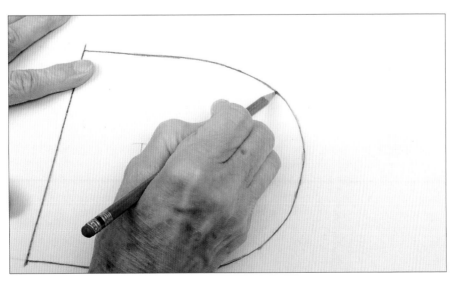

With the number 2 pencil, go over the traced lines to transfer the other side to the cardboard.

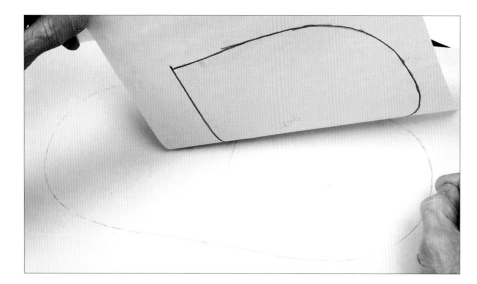

Lift the paper and you will see that you now have a pattern of the top of the entire box.

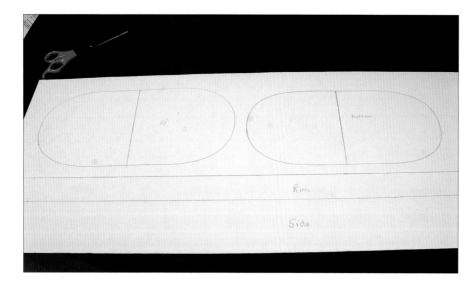

Transfer the bottom of the glove box to the cardboard in the same manner. Measure the rim and side piece as specified along the grain of the cardboard.

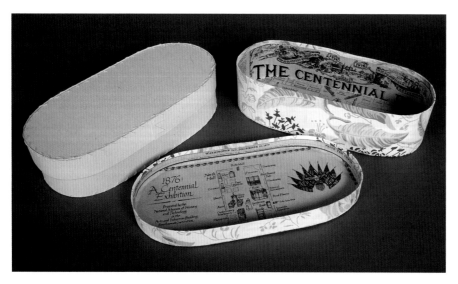

Follow the Basic Skills chapter to complete the box.

Heart Box

Heart boxes were used to hold trinkets, jewelry, ribbons, or lace caps. This project will teach you to sew a different-shaped box. The sewing starts and ends at the bottom point of the heart.

Following the steps in Basic Skills, trace the pattern on the pulp board and cut out the pieces.

Also Needed

- Rim: $^3/_4$ x 15 inches
- Side: 2 x 15 inches

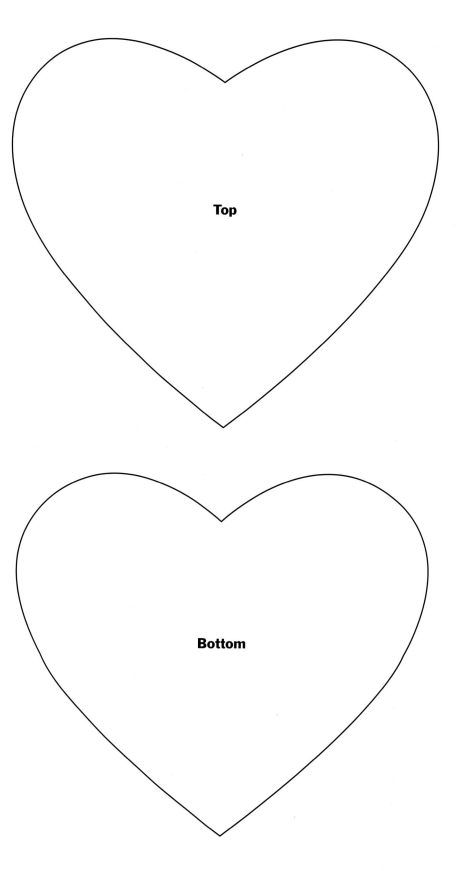

Top

Bottom

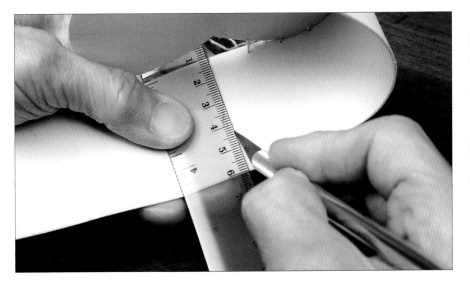

Start sewing at the point of the box. Crease the side piece at the point where it will indent in the center of the heart and mark it. Measure from the end of the side piece to the indentation mark. Using this measurement, mark the top of the side piece. Draw a line between the two marks and score it with a craft knife.

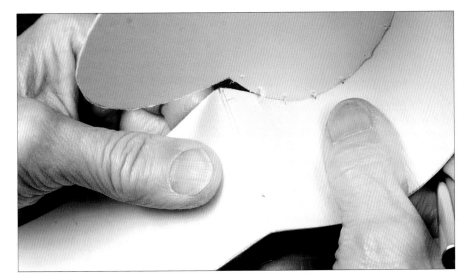

Bend the cardboard.

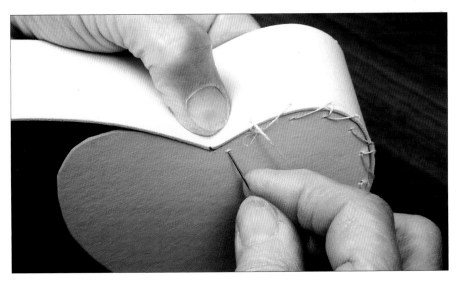

Ease the cardboard to the contour of the heart and sew.

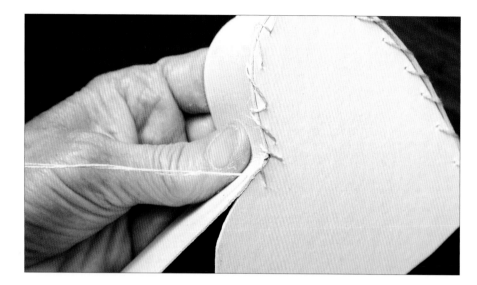

Continue sewing back to the point.

Trim the extra cardboard to make the point flush.

Punch three pairs of holes on either side of the point.

From inside, bring the needle up through the bottom hole and down through the opposite hole.

Take the needle up through the middle hole.

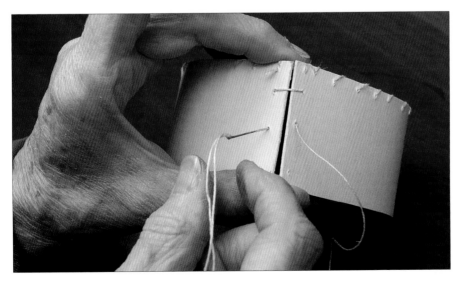

Move the needle across and down through the opposite hole.

Then take it through the top hole.

Move it across to the opposite hole.

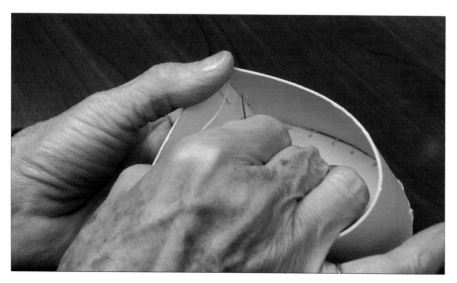

Return by pushing the needle up through the middle hole.

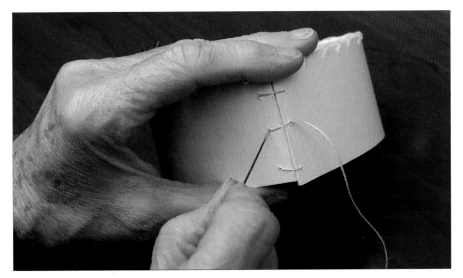

Sew down through the opposite hole.

Then go up through the bottom hole and down the opposite hole.

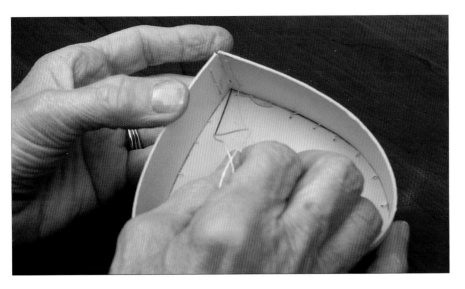

Send the needle through the seam at the bottom.

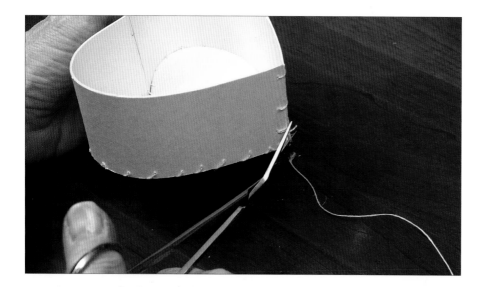

Cut off the thread.

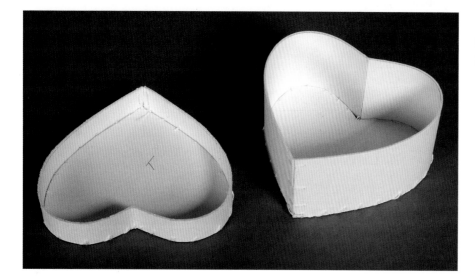

Sew the rim to the top in the same manner.

Cover and line the box as directed in Basic Skills.

Comb Box

These boxes were constructed to hold the decorative combs that were popular in the mid-nineteenth century. There were different sizes and shapes to accommodate specific combs.

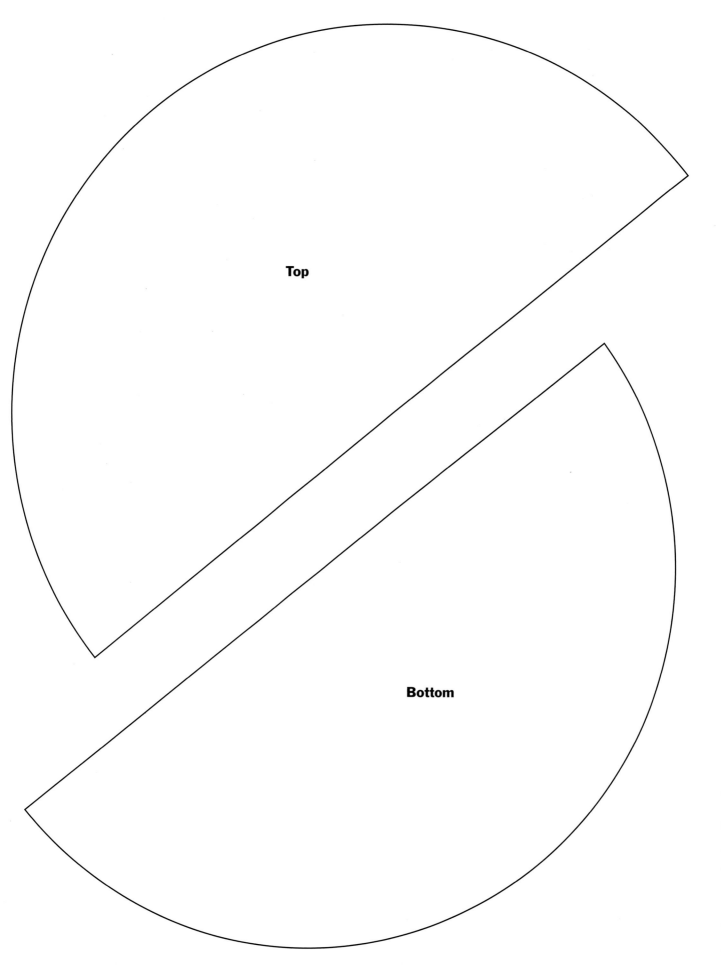

Top

Bottom

Following the steps in Basic Skills, trace the pattern on pulp board and cut out the pieces.

Both the bottom and top are sewn in the same manner, so the following steps apply to both parts.

Also Needed

- Rim: 1 x 22 inches
- Side: 6^1/$_2$ x 22 inches

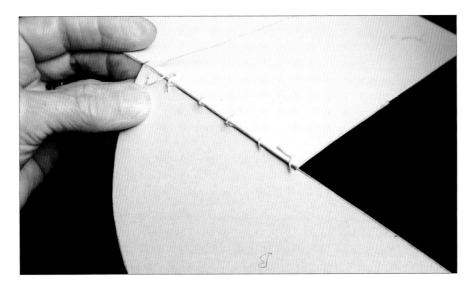

Start sewing at the back of the box.

When you reach the first corner, measure from the point where you began sewing to the point where you stopped. Mark the inches on the side piece at the bottom. Do the same for the rim piece when you sew it and mark the inches on top.

Mark inches on the side piece at the top and the rim strip at the bottom.

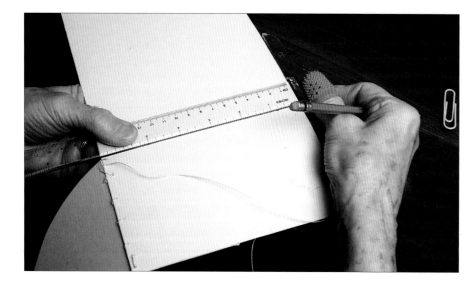

Line up the top and bottom marks with a ruler.

Draw a line.

Score along the line with a craft knife.

Bend to make a sharp corner.

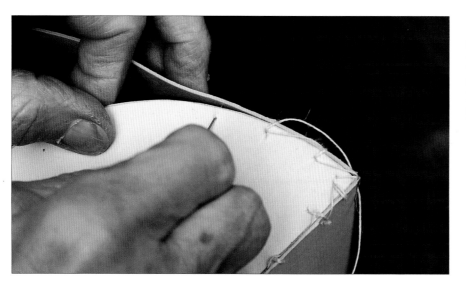

Continue sewing to the next corner. Measure the distance between corners and mark top and bottom. Draw a line and score with a craft knife.

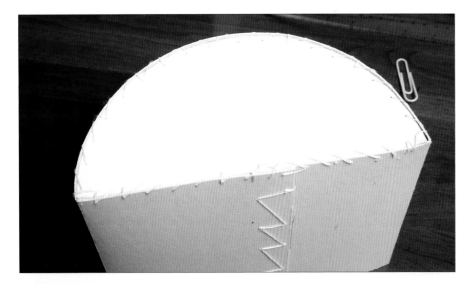

Continue sewing and finish by over-lapping the seam as in Basic Skills.

To finish, follow the methods in Basic Skills for measuring, cutting out the covering, and lining papers and pasting them to the box.

Hexagon Bandbox

Hexagon bandboxes were used for storage and as containers for sewing and art supplies. In making the box, the rim and side pieces are scored to bend easily around the corners.

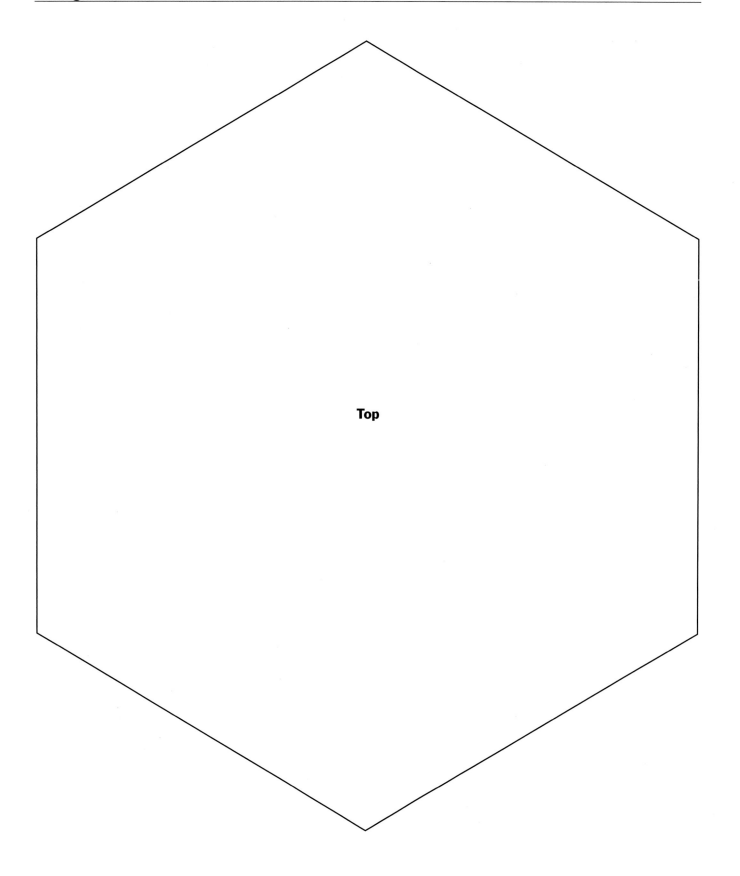

Top

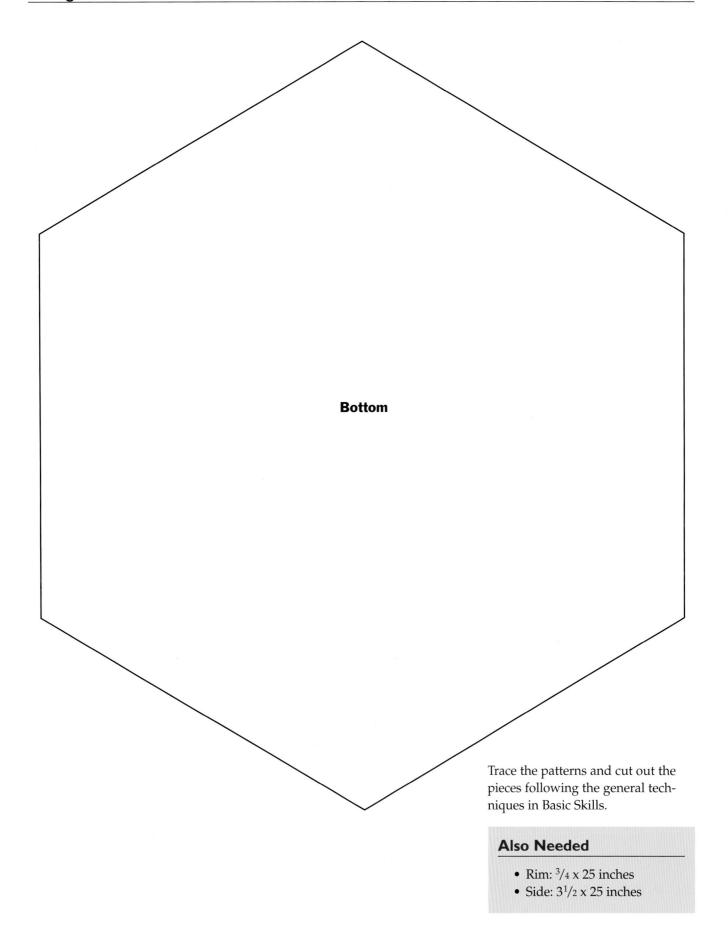

Bottom

Trace the patterns and cut out the pieces following the general techniques in Basic Skills.

Also Needed

- Rim: $^3/_4$ x 25 inches
- Side: $3^1/_2$ x 25 inches

Start sewing the rim at the back of the box.

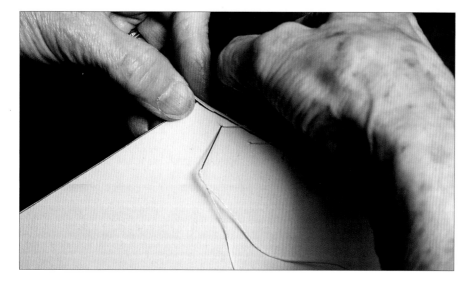

Sew to the first corner.

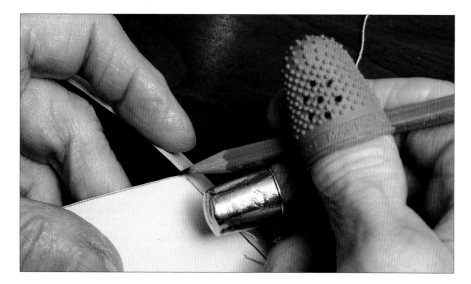

Mark the rim at the corner.

Measure from the point where you started sewing and the part where you stopped.

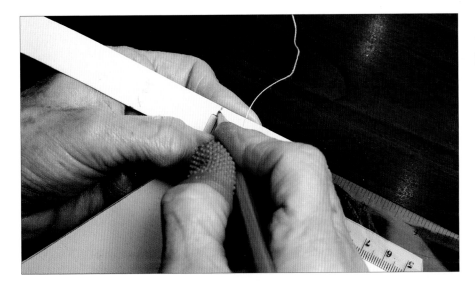

Using the measurement, mark the bottom edge of the rim.

Draw a line.

Score on the line with a craft knife.

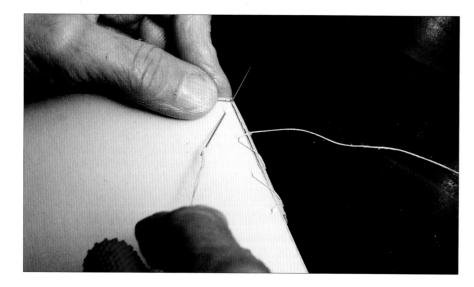

Continue sewing to the next corner.

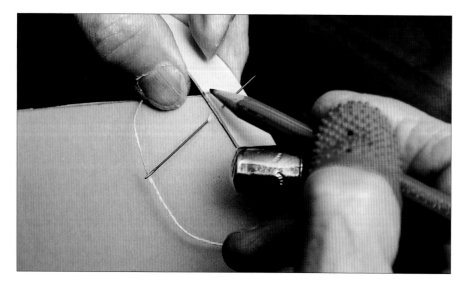

Mark the top of the rim at the corner.

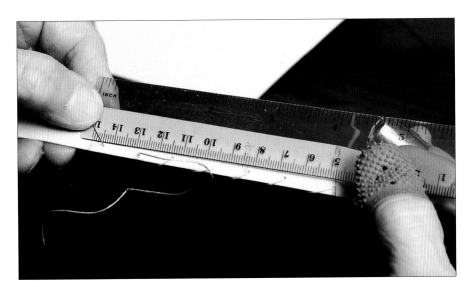

Measure from the first corner.

Mark the bottom of the rim strip and draw a line.

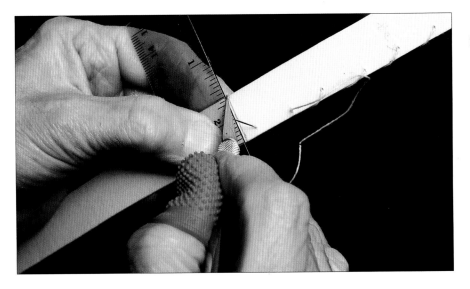

Score on the line with a craft knife.

Continue sewing and scoring corners until you finish the box. Overlap at the end to make a seam as demonstrated in Basic Skills.

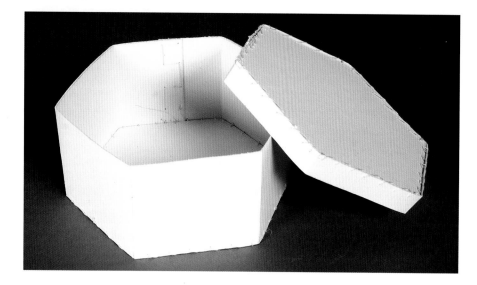

Sew the bottom of the hexagon box in the same manner as the top.

Cover and line the box following the general steps in Basic Skills.

Project 5
Tea Caddy

Tea was a precious commodity during the mid-eighteenth century and early nineteenth century. Special boxes, or tea caddies, were made for storage. Most tea caddies were constructed of wood, porcelain, or metal; however, there were some made of cardboard. This tea caddy has a more complex shape than the boxes you've made so far.

Top

Cut two side pieces

Trace the patterns and cut out the pieces following the steps in Basic Skills. Notice you will need two side pieces.

Also Needed

- Rim: $^3/_4$ x 17 inches
- Middle strip: 3 x 18 inches

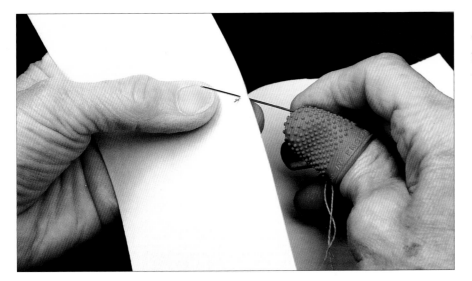

To begin making the bottom of the box, place the knot inside at the center of the long middle strip.

Starting at the center of one side piece, sew it to the long middle strip.

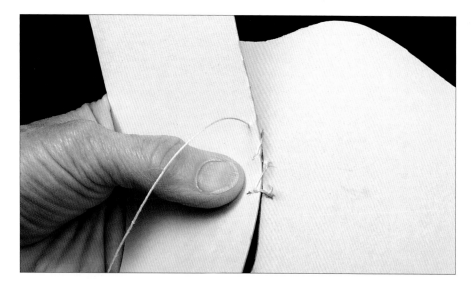

Sew in one direction to the top edge, maintaining the shape of the box.

Ease the strip around the corner.

Continue sewing to the top edge of the box.

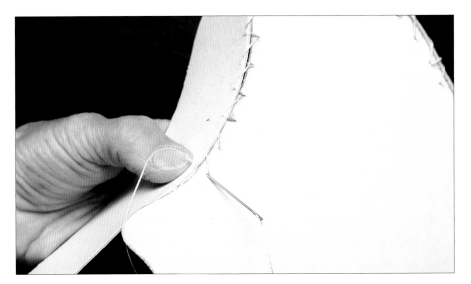

Then go back to the center and sew in the other direction.

Continue sewing to the top edge. Then sew the other side of the strip to the other side of the box in the same manner.

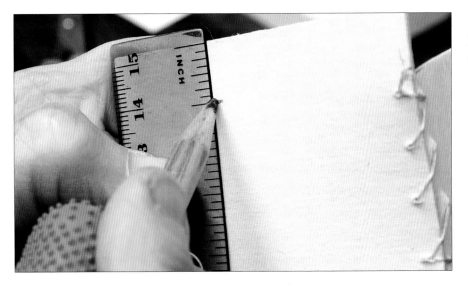

Measure the excess length at the top of each end of the long strip.

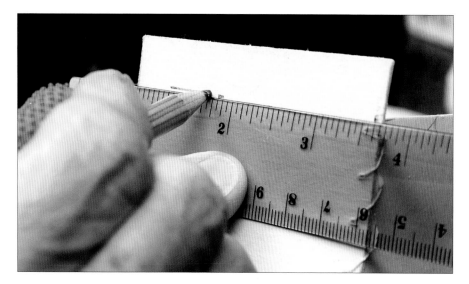

Draw a line.

Cut off the excess at the top of each end so the top edges are even.

To begin making the top of the box, sew the rim to the top starting at the back center of the top piece.

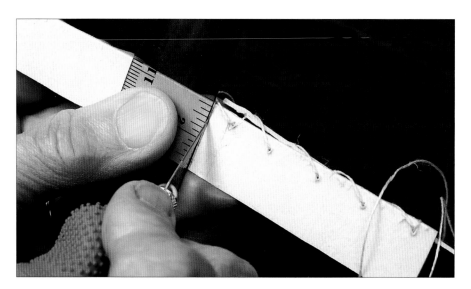

At the corner, score the rim piece on the outside with a craft knife.

Bend the rim around the corner.

Continue sewing, making sharp points at each corner. End by overlapping seams at the back as demonstrated in Basic Skills.

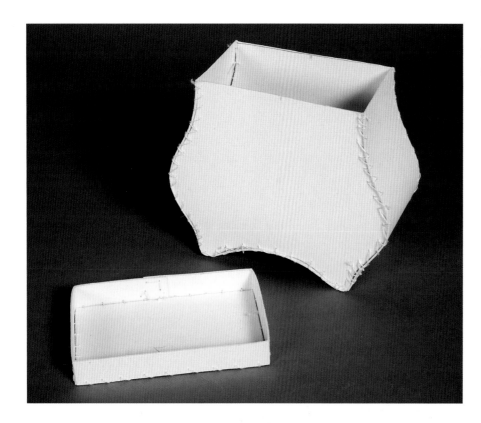

Here is what the box looks like at this point.

To cover the outside bottom of the box, measure and cut out the pieces as follows. Make the two paper side pieces $3/8$ inches wider than the box all around.

The paper strip to cover the middle cardboard between the two sides is $1/4$ inch narrower than the width of the box and 1 inch longer to allow for a $1/2$-inch overlap at each top edge of the box.

For the top and rim coverings, follow the measurements in Basic Skills.

Using a sponge or bristle brush, apply paste to one of the side coverings.

Then apply paste to one side of the box.

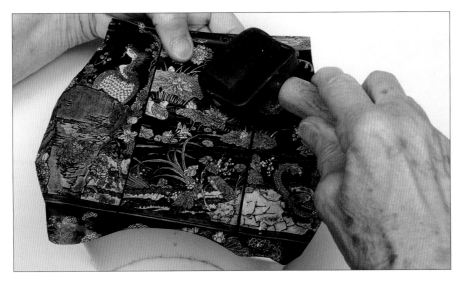

Center the paper so there is an overlap all around the box, and adhere it to the side. Smooth the outside with a seam roller.

Turn the box around with the paper down on the table and smooth on the inside with the roller.

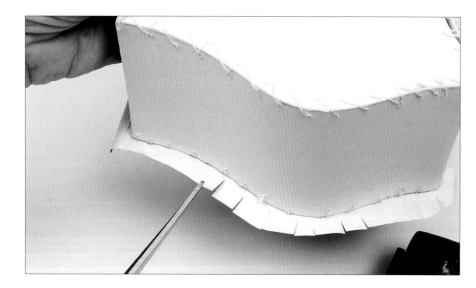

Clip the excess $3/8$-inch paper every $1/2$ inch around the side of the box. Do not clip the top edge of the box. It will be folded over at the end.

Apply paste to the clipped edges of the box.

Fold over and press the paper to the side of the box. Smooth the folded edges with the seam roller.

Paste the other side covering in the same manner.

Clip the top edge of the paper at each corner so it will fold over smoothly.

Apply paste to the paper and the top inside edge of the box.

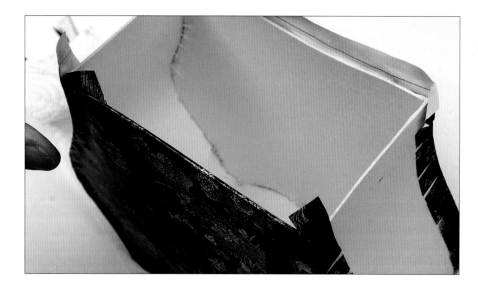

Fold over the top edges.

Apply paste to the long strip covering.

Apply paste to the middle of the box.

Starting at the center of the long strip, adhere it to the middle of the box bottom.

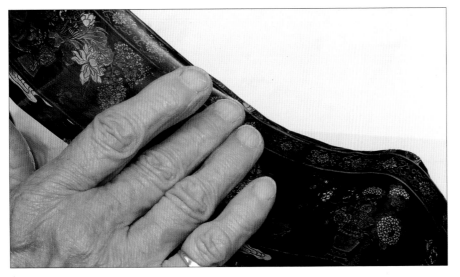

Ease the paper in one direction to the top of the box.

Then ease the paper in the other direction to the top. There should be extra length at the top on both sides.

Smooth the paper out with the seam roller.

Trim the overlap pieces so you have $1/2$ inch extra at each end.

Add paste to the overlap papers and the sections of the box they will cover.

Fold the top edges to the inside of the box.

This is how the box looks at this point.

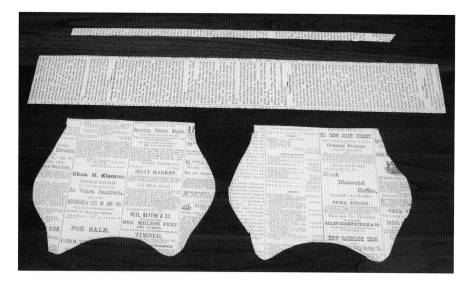

To line the inside of the box, measure and cut out the pieces as follows. Make the two side pieces $1/4$ inch wider around the side edges and $1/4$ inch narrower at the top edges. Cut the long strip $1/2$ inch narrower than the width of the box and $1/2$ inch shorter than the length.

For the inside linings of the top and rim, follow the measurements in Basic Skills.

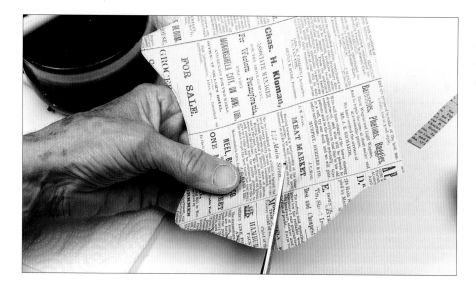

Clip the $1/4$ inch extra width around the side of the newspaper. Do not clip the top edge.

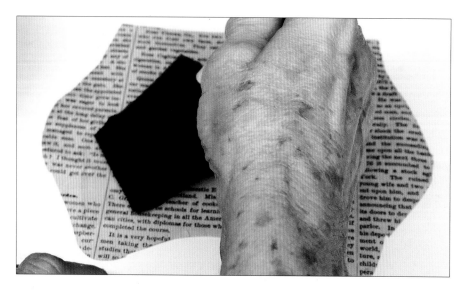

Apply paste to the side piece.

Insert the side piece, easing the clipped edges toward the bottom. Smooth with a seam roller or spatula. Insert the other side piece in the same manner.

Apply paste to the middle strip piece and then to the middle strip inside the box.

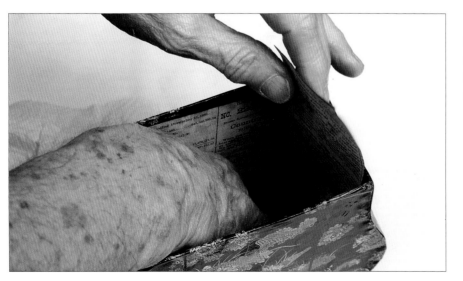

Insert the middle piece 1/4 inch down from the top edge of the box. Clip any excess paper so it is 1/4 inch down from the opposite edge.

The top edges should be even.

Here is the finished box.

Patterns for Additional Bandboxes

This section provides patterns for more boxes. It's now up to you to apply what you've learned in the previous chapters to construct and cover them.

Above: The Bonnet Box is similar to the Glove Box you made previously. The patterns are on the next page.

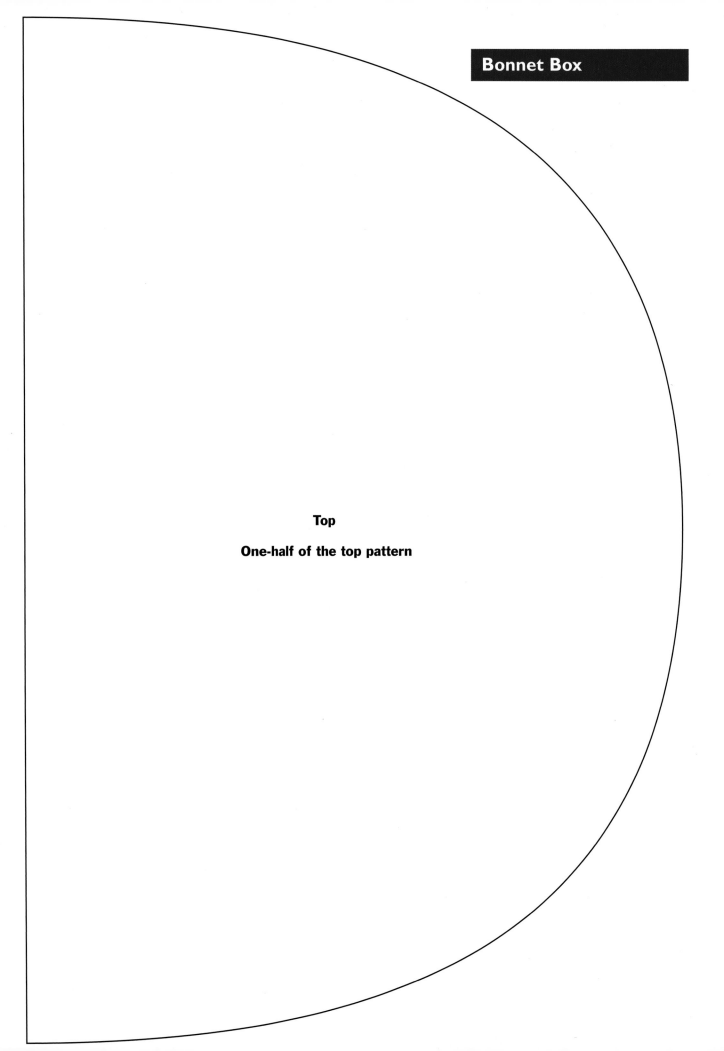

Bonnet Box

Top

One-half of the top pattern

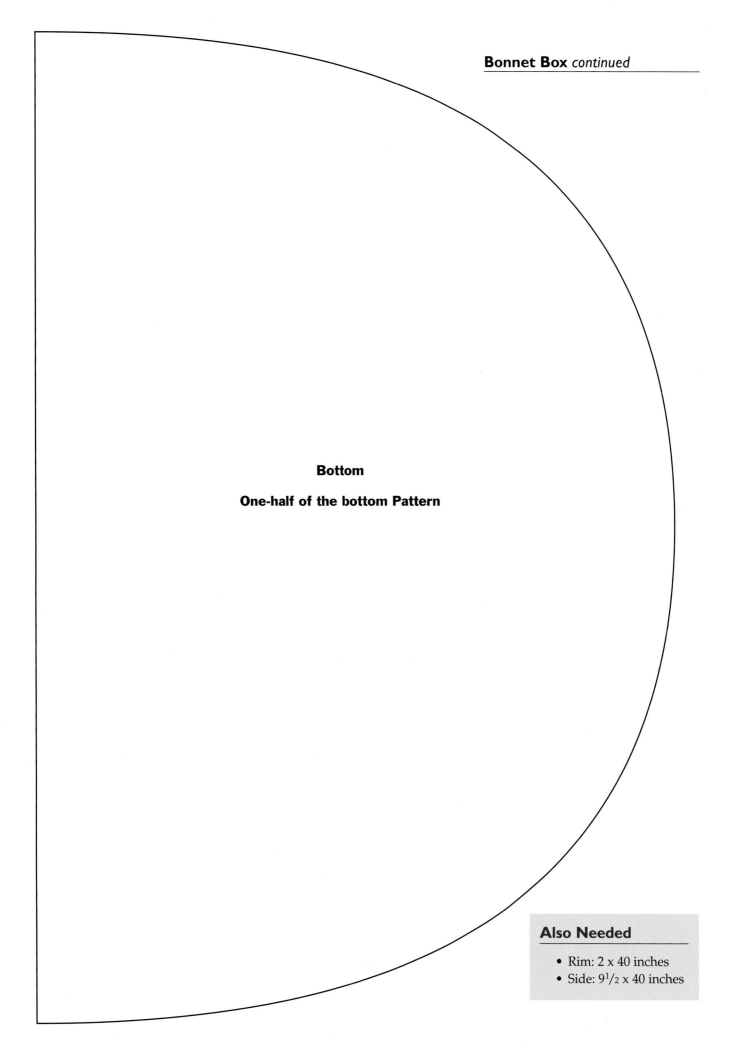

Bottom

One-half of the bottom Pattern

Also Needed

- Rim: 2 x 40 inches
- Side: $9^1/_2$ x 40 inches

The covering used on this sewing box is a historic friendship quilt pattern.

Also Needed

- Rim: $^3/_4$ x 25 inches
- Side: 3 x 25 inches

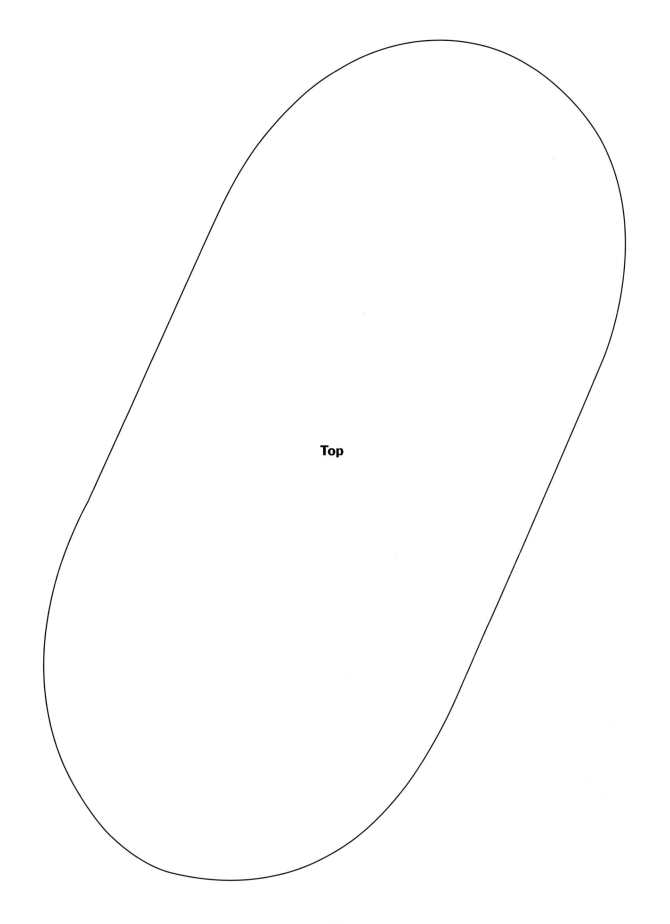

Top

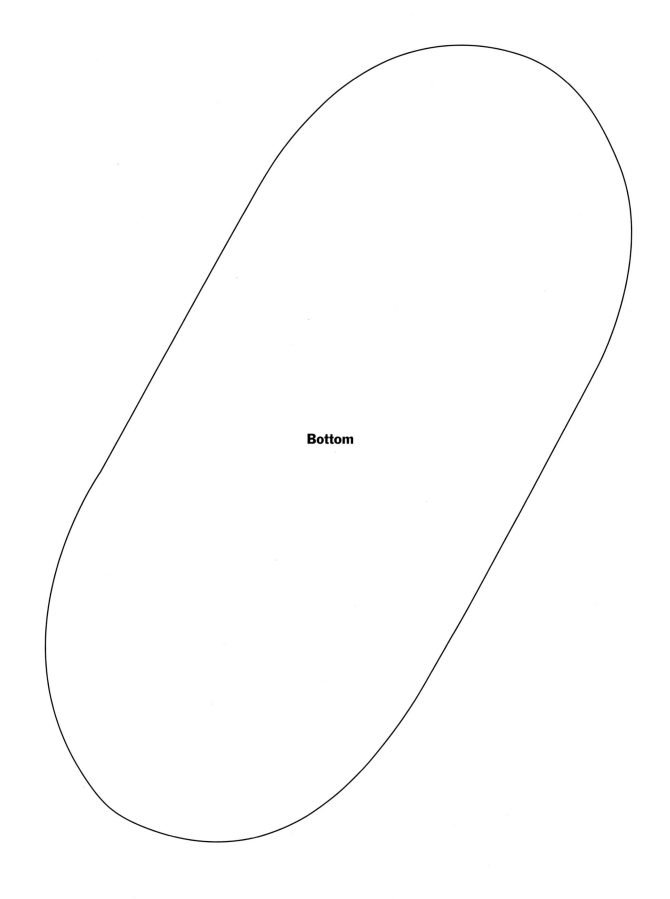

Bottom

Here's a series project of three boxes of different sizes that can be nested. The covering used here is a hand-blocked printed wallpaper.

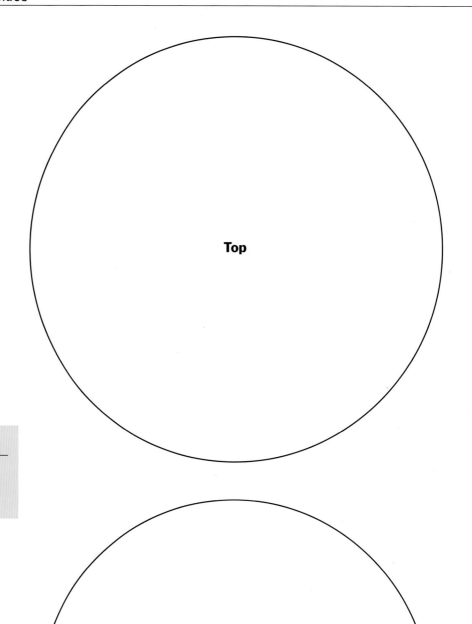

Top

Bottom

SMALL BOX

Also Needed

- Rim: $^3/_4$ x 15 inches
- Side: $2^1/_2$ x 15 inches

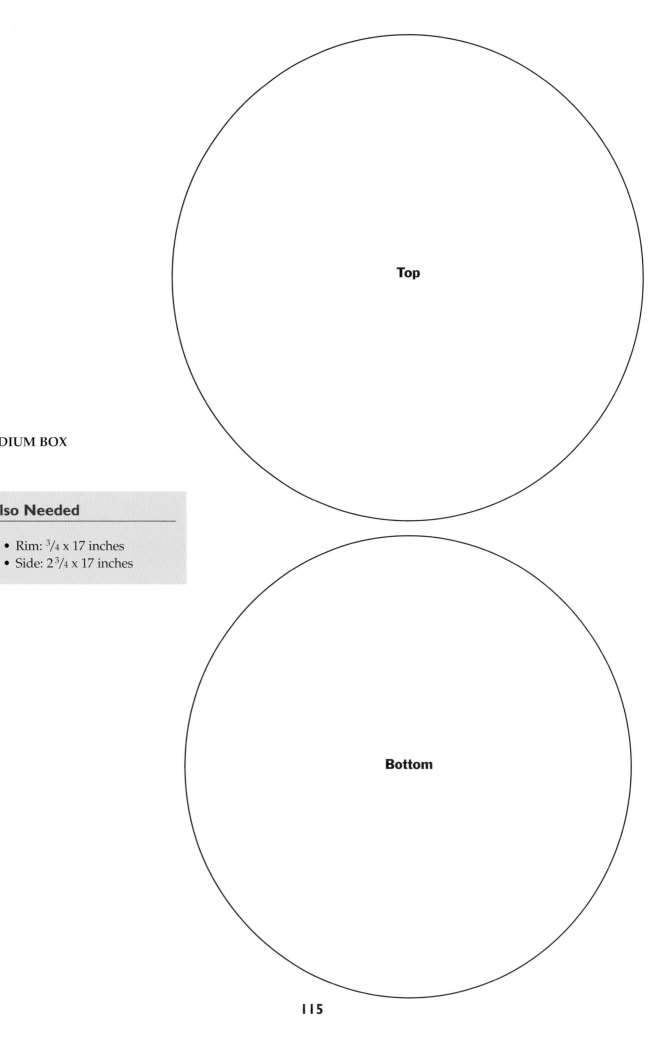

MEDIUM BOX

Also Needed

- Rim: $^3/_4$ x 17 inches
- Side: $2^3/_4$ x 17 inches

Top

Bottom

LARGE BOX

Also Needed

- Rim: 1 x 21 inches
- Side: 3^1/$_2$ x 21 inches

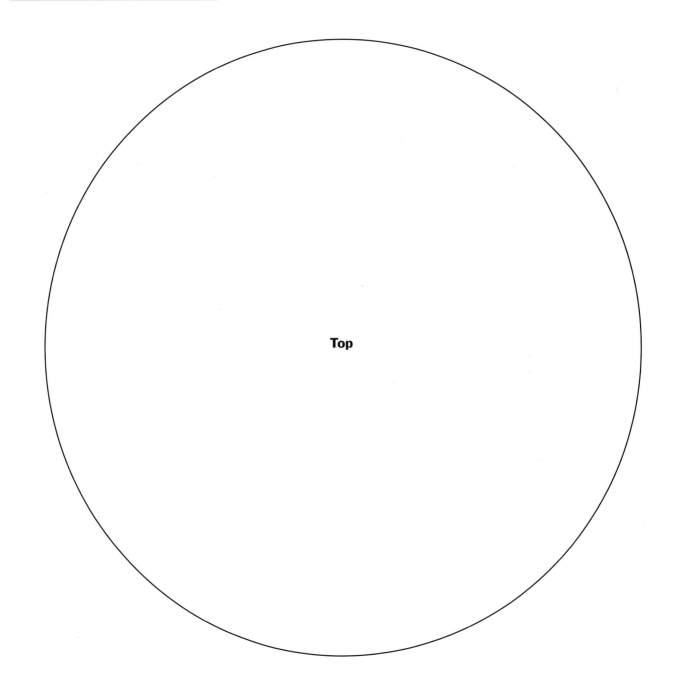

Top

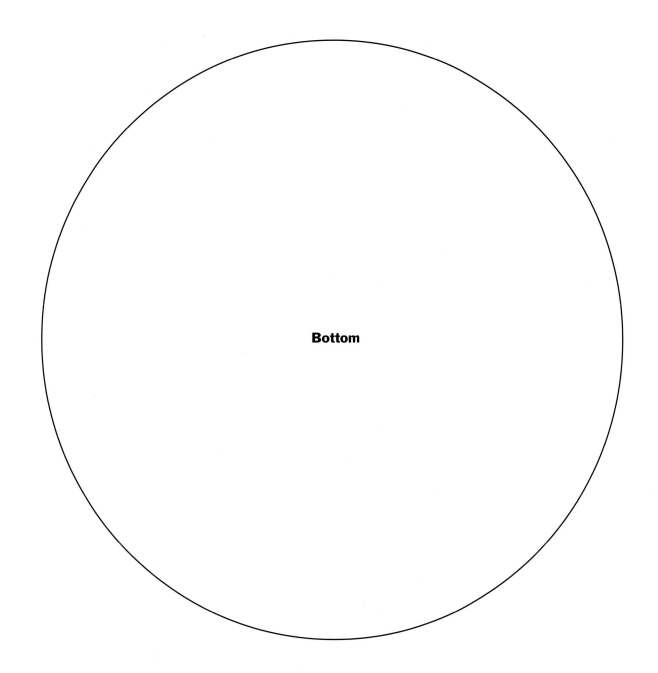

Bottom

Design Your Own Bandbox Pattern

To design a pattern, always make the top of the bandbox $\frac{1}{8}$ inch larger than the bottom. For larger boxes, such as the Bonnet Box, make the top $\frac{3}{16}$ inch larger than the bottom.

Tip

If the length of the cardboard isn't long enough to go around the circumference of a box, join two pieces of cardboard by using the seam-joining technique used in finishing a box.

Ideas for Bandboxes

This section presents an assortment of bandboxes
I've made through the years to give you more ideas
on the varieties of shapes, coverings, and linings that
can be used.

Diamond-shaped bandbox.

COLLECTION OF CATHERINE CHOLMELEY-JONES

The shape of this box was inspired by the hearts used on Pennsylvania Dutch fraktur.

Heart-shaped pinbox and thimble box.

Dollhouse bonnet bandbox and bridesbox covered with miniature wallpaper.

The wallpaper on this bandbox features historic buildings in Philadelphia. COLLECTION OF ART AND JANE MYERS

The newspaper lining the bottom of this box is from August 16, 1945, announcing the end of World War II. COLLECTION OF ART AND JANE MYERS

Another box with lining from an August 16, 1945, newspaper, displaying events during the declaration of peace. COLLECTION OF ART AND JANE MYERS

The 1970 newspaper lining in the top of this bandbox features three-year-old Jodi Myers in the one-hundred-year-old carriage used by her parents to squire her around town. COLLECTION OF ART AND JANE MYERS

The bottom of this bandbox is lined with a 1970 newspaper showing a display of antique kitchen utensils in the Myers family kitchen. COLLECTION OF ART AND JANE MYERS

This memory box has a school emblem on the top and is lined with a commencement announcement inside. COLLECTION OF CATHERINE CHOLMELEY-JONES

Theorem painter Linda Brubaker stenciled the bear design on this box. COLLECTION OF E. CAROLYN HAZELL

A rocking horse theorem, another by Linda Brubaker, is applied to the top of this bandbox. COLLECTION OF LINDA BRUBAKER

A bandbox covered with an English paper titled "The Lamplighter" by Jean Gilder.
COLLECTION OF DANTE CHOLMELEY-JONES

Christmas ornament boxes. COLLECTION OF ART AND JANE MYERS

Bandbox ornaments displayed on a Christmas tree. COLLECTION OF ART AND JANE MYERS

Gallery of Early Bandboxes

H ere is a selection of nineteenth-century bandboxes to give you ideas for making reproductions of authentic pieces.

Above: *This bandbox was made specially to accommodate a man's top hat.* LANDIS VALLEY MUSEUM, PENNSYLVANIA HISTORICAL AND MUSEUM COMMISSION

The newspaper lining in this band-box is dated 1829. It is covered with machine-printed wallpaper. LANDIS VALLEY MUSEUM, PENNSYLVANIA HISTORICAL AND MUSEUM COMMISSION

These bandboxes belonged to Anna Margaret Diller Kinzer, the maternal grandmother of Henry and George Landis, founders of Landis Valley Museum in Lancaster, Pennsylvania. The large box is lined with an 1829 newspaper. The smaller box has a pincushion top covered with a theorem, stenciled with the name "Sarah" and dated 1790. LANDIS VALLEY MUSEUM, PENNSYLVANIA HISTORICAL AND MUSEUM COMMISSION

This large bandbox with oak leaves printed on the wallpaper covering is dated 1835. LITITZ MUSEUM, LITITZ HISTORICAL FOUNDATION

This bandbox is covered and lined with several different papers. This is an example of how a crafter used any scraps of paper he or she could find. LANDIS VALLEY MUSEUM, PENNSYLVANIA HISTORICAL AND MUSEUM COMMISSION

Papers with leaves on a blue background were prevalent on bandboxes during this period. This one is dated 1838. LANDIS VALLEY MUSEUM, PENNSYLVANIA HISTORICAL AND MUSEUM COMMISSION

The theorem covering the velvet lid on this pincushion bandbox includes the sentiment "Think of me." LANDIS VALLEY MUSEUM, PENNSYLVANIA HISTORICAL AND MUSEUM COMMISSION

SUPPLIES AND RESOURCES

A. C. Moore
www.acmoore.com

The Art Store
29 E. King St.
Lancaster, PA 17602
717-394-4600
One-ply pulp board
Marbled paper

Dick Blick Art Materials
P.O. Box 1267
Galesburg, IL 61402-1267
800-828-4548
www.dickblick.com
Four-ply or six-ply posterboard
Marbled paper

Jo-Ann Fabric and Craft Stores
www.joann.com
Sewing supplies

The Mannings
1132 Green Ridge Rd.
P.O. Box 687
East Berlin, PA 17316
800-233-7166
www.the-mannings.com
One-ply linen thread

Michael's
www.michaels.com

MUSEUMS AND HISTORIC SITES

American Folk Art Museum
45 W. 53rd St.
New York, NY 10019
212-265-1040
www.folkartmuseum.org

Cooper-Hewitt National Design Museum
2 E. 91st St.
New York, NY 10128
212-849-8400
www.cooperhewitt.org

Jaffrey Historical Society
Civic Center
41 Main St.
Jaffrey, NH 03452

Landis Valley Museum
2451 Kissel Hill Rd.
Lancaster, PA 17601
717-569-0401
www.landisvalleymuseum.org

Lititz Museum
137-145 E. Main St.
Lititz, PA 17543
717-627-4636
www.lititzhistoricalfoundation.com

Mercer Museum
84 S. Pine St.
Doylestown, PA 18901-4999
215-345-0210
www.mercermuseum.org

Melville Academy Museum
Blackberry Lane and Thorndike Pond Rd.
Jaffrey, NH 03452
www.jcvis.org/museum/museum.php

Phillips Museum of Art
Franklin and Marshall College
College Ave.
Lancaster, PA
717-291-3879
www.fandm.edu/phillipsmuseum.xml

Shelburne Museum
U. S. Route 7
Shelburne, VT 05482
802-985-3346
www.shelburnemuseum.org

BIBLIOGRAPHY

Carlisle, Lillian Baker. *Hat Boxes and Bandboxes at the Shelburne Museum*. Shelburne, VT: Shelburne Museum, 1960.

Greysmith, Brenda. *Wallpaper*. New York: MacMillan, 1976.

Hunter, Dard. *Papermaking*. New York: Dover, 1978.

Kolb, Brenda Waldron, and Lelia Gray Neil. *American Country Christmas*. Birmingham, AL: Oxmoor House, 1994.

Little, Nina Fletcher. *Neat and Tidy*. New York: E. P. Dutton, 1980.

McCalls Needlework and Crafts. Vol. 23, No. 1. (Spring 1978).

McClellan, Mary Elizabeth. *Felt, Silk, and Straw Handmade Hats*. Doylestown, PA: Bucks County Historical Society, 1977.

Rogers, Cory W. "Bandbox Papers at the Shelburne Museum." *Antiques and Fine Art* (Summer 2006), pp. 138–141.

Robinson, Margaret C. *Hannah Davis, A Pioneer Maker of Bandboxes*. Reprint from the *Boston Evening Transcript*, 14 November 1925. Jaffrey, NH: Jaffrey Historical Society, June 1977.

Ross, Pat. *Hannah's Fancy Notions*. New York: Puffin Books, 1992.

———. *To Have and to Hold*. New York: Penguin Books, 1991.

Van Roojen, Pepin. *Decorated Paper Designs*. Amsterdam, The Netherlands: Pepin Press, 1997.